The Pace of Peace

The Pace of Peace

How to Navigate Struggles in
Your Body, Soul, and Home

MICHELLE BRUMGARD

The Pace of Peace: How to Navigate Struggles in Your Body, Soul, and Home

Published By Brumgard Ministries

P.O. Box 125
Abbottstown, PA 17301

Edited by Kerry Harger
Cover Art Design by Levi Matthews
Exterior/Interior Design by Alli Prince
Printed in the United States of America.
First Edition: January 2026
ISBN: 979-8-9932753-0-7 (paperback)
ISBN: 979-8-9932753-1-4 (eBook)
For more information, visit: www.michellebrumgard.com

To my husband, Luke - thank you for loving me so well.

Table of Contents

Introduction: Becoming a Woman of Peace

IN THE DARK OF NIGHT, the kids and my husband are asleep. I slowly crawl out of my bed so I don't wake him. I get on my knees by the side of my bed. The tears begin to trickle down my face. I don't even know where to begin. The overwhelm is like a thick, heavy blanket laid over me. My head drops to the floor and into my hands; my knees ache as I bend forward. The pull and pain in my legs are too much. My body aches, and I decide to lie flat on my stomach. With my hands laid flat on the floor and my forehead resting on the backs of them, I cry.

"Dear God, help me? I'm so tired of being tired. Everything hurts. Luke doesn't understand. The kids are just getting by. I'm so tired of all the drama in our family. Oh dear God, help. I'm so tired of being tired. Tired of being misunderstood. Tired of being the strong one to hold it all together. Why me? Will you ever give me a break? Why aren't you answering my prayers?"

From my perspective, I was failing. Our home was never clean enough. The constant clutter overwhelmed me. There was continuous family drama I was navigating. My body seemed to hate me. I knew I should be eating healthier and working out. I should be meal planning for all of us to eat better and feel better.

As a homeschooling family, my kids' education seemed adequate, and yet I still couldn't help but compare them to others. However, we had three goals for their home education: Did they have a love for learning? Did they love the Lord? Were they alive? Whatever form of education a child receives, they will have gaps. Ultimately, when I reviewed these goals, we were doing okay.

Why couldn't I be thankful? Why couldn't I be content? I'm so blessed. I know better. I should do better were a few more of the thoughts that flooded my mind as my hands muffled the sobs. It was a miracle that my gut-wrenching cry didn't wake Luke with the snotty, tear-filled mess I was on the floor. After pouring out my self-pity to the Lord and releasing all the held-back tears, I quietly crawled back into bed after praying for sleep that would restore my overwhelmed and exhausted self.

By morning, I would wake and go about my day. Whenever I would leave the home, my life appeared completely put together. My loving husband worked hard to provide for the family and helped with cooking and house chores. Our kids were well-behaved and "easy kids," as one mom once said to me. I was the dependable and consistent one whom others brought their prayer requests. It was my honor and delight to pray for others. I always had great faith for God to answer my prayers for others.

Prayers for myself, I have to be honest, seemed to lack the same depth of belief that God would intervene on my behalf. Often, I would be like the father with the demon-possessed son in Mark 9:24: "Immediately the father of the child cried out and said, 'I believe; help my unbelief!'"

Looking back through my old journals, the theme clearly shines through on each page. I poured out the anxious thoughts, the fears that gripped me, the relationships that continually disappointed me, and how I didn't feel "good enough." Often, I felt misunderstood as I wrote within the pages, processing my life. Time and time again, my written prayers petitioned God for peace. Peace in my body. Peace in my soul. Peace in my home and relationships. I knew the Prince of Peace and prayed for guidance and breakthrough while navigating all my feelings.

As I look back at these prayers, the journey appears clear now. In the process of these last several years, I was finding my pace of peace. A pace that is rooted in Peace Himself and unique to me. Peace is a person. Peace is a product of His Spirit in my life as I abide in Jesus Christ.

Chaos and overwhelm are not our portion as followers of Christ. Through these pages, my stories will reveal snapshots of who I was and the process of becoming a woman of Peace. Each chapter will give you a practice to explore and implement, along with a thought to cultivate. I suggest you read a chapter a day or through these pages as quickly as you want. Then go back and DO a chapter a week or a chapter a month. Pick the pace that fits your schedule and capacity to implement the practices. In becoming a woman of peace, you will celebrate progress over perfection in the journey. Struggles will cease to overwhelm you. With Holy Spirit, you will find that, by abiding in Christ, you will live at your own unique pace of peace.

As you embark on this journey, I pray Paul's prayer for spiritual strength to the church of Ephesus found in Ephesians 3:14-21:

"For this reason I bow my knees before the Father, from whom every family in heaven and on earth is named, that according to the riches of his glory he may grant you to be strengthened with power through his Spirit in your inner being, so that Christ may dwell in your hearts through faith—that you, being rooted and grounded in love, may have strength to comprehend with all the saints what is the breadth and length and height and depth, and to know the love of Christ that surpasses knowledge, that you may be filled with all the fullness of God. Now to him who is able to do far more abundantly than all that we ask or think, according to the power at work within us, to him be the glory in the church and in Christ Jesus throughout all generations, forever and ever. Amen."

With Christ, you will become a woman of peace.

With Peace,
You are Known

Meet Peace Himself

For to us a child is born, to us a son is given; and the government shall be upon his shoulder, and his name shall be called Wonderful Counselor, Mighty God, Everlasting Father, Prince of Peace. - Isaiah 9:6

OUR PASTOR KNELT BESIDE ME, holding a little booklet of colors. It was made of cardboard, and each page was a simple, singular color. No words. He used this tool to offer me hope and a future found in Christ. With each turn of the page, a color represented a portion of the teaching and an invitation to come to Christ. If you grew up in an evangelical church background, you are probably familiar with these colors used in booklets, on bracelets, and a multitude of evangelist tools. Black: to discuss how we are all sinful in nature and have fallen short of the glory of God. Red: to represent the blood of Jesus Christ on the cross and His sacrificial love for us. White: to show the purity available to us when we repent of our sins. Jesus would cleanse me of these sins. Finally, gold or yellow: to represent the promise of eternal life in Heaven.

It's interesting to think back and wonder if I remember the time of receiving Christ as my Savior accurately. In my then seven-year-old self, I can recall the offer of salvation giving me hope. A hope that there was a place of peace in my future. The hope that God would come and make everything better in my broken world: a dysfunctional home, a body that was often scared of all the unknowns, and a mind too undeveloped to know what to think.

Hundreds of years before Jesus was born, Isaiah prophesied that Jesus was coming. He was and is the Prince of Peace. With Christ, we are reconciled. When I repented of my sins and accepted Christ as my Savior, I received Peace Himself. Recognizing the peace Christ offered me took years to understand fully. Diagnoses of anxiety, depression, and post-traumatic stress disorder would validate my lack of peace. Jesus was my non-judging, always forgiving best friend. I never abandoned my faith, but there was very little evidence of it during my teens and early twenties. Marrying at 23 and having our first child nine months later, I began to draw near to God again. Eventually, my faith began to grow exponentially, but I still felt like something was missing.

Jesus was my non-judging, always forgiving best friend.

There's one particular woman in the Bible, who I believe would've related to me. She probably felt misunderstood and like something was missing in her life, too, until the day she met the Prince of Peace. We don't know much about her, but the details of her life paint a picture of a woman in search of something. She had multiple husbands, five to be exact, as the Word tells us in John 4:18. Did these husbands die? Is this why she remarried frequently? I wonder if she had any children. Or, could she not have children, and was that why she was disregarded as a wife? We know she was a Samaritan woman going to get water from the well alone in the heat of the day. I've heard it said that the fact that she was alone is probably indicative of her shame and the judgment of others towards her. In my mind's eye, I see her carrying her vessel for water towards the well. I imagine her thinking through her day, the things she needs to do, what she should do differently, better, and all the "if onlys." If only she could do ______. Fill in the blank with a multitude of possibilities that bring shame, guilt, and condemnation.

There was a man sitting at the well. He turns toward her, not with condemnation but a question. This man, Jesus, asks her for a drink of water. "The Samaritan woman said to him, 'You are a Jew and I am a Samaritan woman. How can you ask me for a drink?'" (John 4:9). Jews customarily did not acknowledge or speak to Samaritans. The conversation continued as she drew up water for Jesus. He shares that He has a living water that will quench her thirst, unlike the physical water she will yearn for again. In their brief conversation, she recognizes Jesus must be a prophet, for He knew she had been married multiple times. She acknowledges the coming Messiah. Jesus reveals Himself to her: "Then Jesus declared, 'I, the one speaking to you—I am he'" (John 4:26 NIV[1]).

[1] *Holy Bible: New International Version* (Grand Rapids, MI: Zondervan, 2011).

The Samaritan woman was known by Christ, and so are you, my friend. Jesus intentionally chose to go through Samaria in his journey to Galilee. I imagine He was waiting for her, knowing she was coming, and made Himself available to reveal Himself to her. He saw past her sin, past her history, past her shame, and spoke to the longing deep within her for the living water only He could offer.

The Samaritan woman was known by Christ, and so are you, my friend.

Take a moment and contemplate how you can reorient your days to intentionally encounter Christ yourself. He's already there, willing and ready to listen and speak to you. Your unique encounter time doesn't need to look like anyone else's encounter. The Church has told us to have "quiet time" daily, reading our Bibles, praying, and contemplating His word. Today, I want to set you free to embrace a new thought with the question, "How will I encounter Christ today?" What will I bring into this encounter time? What will I do or not do?

In 2015, I attended a group fitness instructor training retreat with Revelation Wellness, a non-profit ministry that trains people to love God and their bodies. In my prayers leading up to the retreat, I told God I knew something was missing, but I didn't know what was missing. It's okay to confess to God that you don't feel like you are encountering Him. It's okay to admit that something just feels off and you don't know what.

Ask and He will deliver. In this particular circumstance, everything changed at the end of one workout. We were rolling up our mats, and the founder of Revelation Wellness, Alisa Keeton, was at the back of the room. She asked everyone to pause for a moment as she believed she had a word for someone in the room. As Alisa began to describe this picture she was seeing in her mind's eye, I began to feel my heart flutter, my palms sweat, and a bit of uneasiness in my stomach. It was as if the Holy Spirit was saying through my body, "Listen up, this is for you." She began to describe an old red pickup truck. It was a farm truck driving through fields, a dad and his daughter inside. The image she described was like a movie of my childhood playing in my mind. Then, Alisa shared her interpretation of what God was showing her:

"God wants this daughter in the room to know that she can let her hair down. Unlike her earthly father, God the Father will never disappoint you. He understands you and knows you. With Him, you are safe."

Honestly, I don't remember everything Alisa spoke about as she described this image. The tears began to fall as soon as she mentioned the old red farm truck. I didn't fully understand what was happening. All I knew was that I couldn't deny what I was experiencing. For the first time in my life, I recognized I was a daughter of God. My Heavenly Father, through Alisa, let me know what was missing: I had a disconnect with the Father in the Holy Trinity.

Jesus had been my best friend since I asked him into my

heart at that tender age of 7. I recognized that I was a sinner: the black in the little booklet all those years ago. Jesus came and paid the ultimate price for my sins, washing my soul white as it was described. I received new life in repentance of my sins to Christ, represented in the color green. One day, I will spend eternity in Heaven represented in yellow. Jesus never left me, even though I often ignored Him through the years. The Holy Spirit became the quiet whisper of conviction. I believe those whispers saved my life many times as a teenager when I strayed away from the religion I knew as a child. In rebellion, I sought to be loved, seen, and known through school achievements, relationships with boys, alcohol abuse, and more. But I didn't really know God as my Father until this moment. I knew Jesus was part of a Holy Trinity with the Holy Spirit and the Father. To be a daughter of God to Jesus, to the Holy Spirit, and to the Father? I hadn't known that type of intimate relationship. This moment with God became a mountain-top encounter that changed everything from that day forward.

Encounter time is where I have been established as a woman of peace

Encounter time is where I have been established as a woman of peace who is able to live at a pace of peace. I invite you to join me in encountering God in your everyday life. At the end of each chapter, I will offer you P.E.A.C.E. This acronym is a part of who I am and what I now live: **prayer**, exploring possibilities by **elevating my**

perspective, asking good questions of myself and others, **cultivating new thoughts** intentionally, and **embodying the Truth** of who God says I am in physical practices. I invite you to explore these practices moving forward as options for you to encounter God afresh. Briefly visit each in this moment, or go deep into each immediately. My hope and prayer is that these P.E.A.C.E. portions will be anchors of your journey that you can continually revisit and discover new layers to the invitations within them. Recognize your capacity in this moment and at least read through the invitation in each step — allow the seeds to be planted for P.E.A.C.E.

Pause and Pray:

Take a deep breath. Roll your shoulders up and back with another deep breath. Read this prayer that I am praying for you as I write. It is still true today as you read it.

Father God, I smile in delight for this precious friend reading these words. I may not know her, but you do. I am so grateful for her desire to become a woman of peace. Today, as she reads these words, I pray that you would encounter her afresh. Would you please highlight to her any areas of disconnect with you as her Heavenly Father, Jesus Christ as her Savior, and Holy Spirit as her helper? I pray that she would have dreams and encounter your Word in ways that minister to her heart, establishing or re-establishing who she is as your daughter, friend, and companion. In Jesus' mighty name, amen.

Elevate Your Perspective and Explore Possibilities:

I invite you to begin to explore how you relate to each person of the Holy Trinity: Father, Son, and Holy Spirit. Explore each of these relationships and notice if any of them feel uncomfortable. In my experience, I have seen many people relate to the Father as they relate to their earthly father. Recognize this and have no shame. Jesus, the Son of God, is typically the easiest to relate to as a best friend. Yet, we can disconnect from the Truth of the sacrificial love he lived out perfectly. Jesus was fully man and lived in this broken world in the flesh. Explore how you relate to the life He lived, died, and resurrected for you and me. He then gave us the gift of the Holy Spirit, which may seem a bit surreal or confusing. Each of us has a different experience in our faith walk with each person of the Holy Trinity. It's okay. Examine your relationship with each one and how you can encounter them each day. Notice and explore any disconnects, negative emotions that come up, or areas of curiosity that arise as you sit with each of them.

Ask a Question:

Invite God to help you with your relationship with Him. I knew something was missing, and I believe He will answer your prayer for any place you may feel disconnected, too. As you pray and seek, you are welcome to ask questions of each person of the Holy Trinity. In this section of our peace acronym, I invite you to sit down with a journal and pen. Let whatever comes to your mind out on the page through your writing. I will give you 3-5 questions to begin reflecting on.

"Father God, how do I relate to you? Jesus, how do I relate to you? Holy Spirit, how do I relate to you?" Today, you have permission to get curious about how you can deepen and strengthen your relationship with our mighty God, three in one, by asking questions.

Cultivate a Thought:

This is a thought you may want to put on a sticky note on your bathroom mirror, your Bible, or another place you see frequently. In a later chapter, I will teach you the process I use to get to these kinds of thoughts. For now, I will offer you thoughts to practice that are from my journey. Here is the first thought you can cultivate: *The Prince of Peace sees, knows, hears, and loves me today, in this moment, as I am.*

Embody Truth:

Evaluate your days and how you can get in your physical body while you encounter God. When I say "get in your body," I mean to recognize how you are feeling, name what you are feeling, and where you feel it in your body. A key component in becoming a woman of peace is strengthening the connection between God, your body, and your soul (your mind, will, and emotions). The first step of deepening this connection is to evaluate your thoughts and feelings in each of these areas. Embody Truth this week by turning on a worship song or an audible Bible recording as you fold laundry, wash dishes, take a walk, or do any regular activity. God is ready to be with you in the mundane and ordinary to take the overwhelm and bring you peace. With the Prince of Peace, you are known and accepted.

Look for Evidence

I will remember the deeds of the LORD; yes, I will remember your wonder of old. I will ponder all your work, and meditate on your mighty deeds. - Psalm 77:11&12

PAIN RADIATED DOWN MY LEGS with each step on the gravel section of the Flat Rock hiking trail. Luke and our two kids were walking in front of me and frequently turned back to check on me. My breath was labored, and frustration was evident in my attitude. We were on one of our first hikes as a family, as Luke and I prepared to hike the Grand Canyon later that fall. In six months, we planned to hike from the North Rim down into the canyon and out the other side to the South Rim. Here I was, struggling to hike up what would be a hill in comparison. It felt like my body was failing me. I desperately tried to think positively and pray with each step. It wasn't going so well. I looked up to see my family moving ahead on the trail with what appeared to be ease. It made me mad. Mad at them. Mad at myself. Mad at God. I questioned so much about my choice to embark on this hard adventure of hiking the Grand Canyon.

The evidence I was compiling told me I would not be able to do it. When we hit a flat gravel section after climbing a bunch of rock steps, I had to stop to catch my breath. Again. The woman with the issue of blood in the Bible came to my mind. I sighed. Luke turned towards me, and my tears fought for release. I finally spoke aloud that I was struggling in my body and in my mind. He hugged me, and I crumbled into tears. For years, I had been circling mountains of defeat in my body. All the way back to my childhood, I had regular stomach aches and headaches, wore heart monitors in search of what was "wrong," was diagnosed as epileptic, undiagnosed as epileptic, and on and on. I could write a book about the struggles in my body alone. This one will only graze the surface. However, I understand now that my body was attempting to tell my story. It carried emotional pain, stored up years of unprocessed emotions, and at the root, longed to be loved and at peace. Oh, how I longed for peace in my body.

This is the peace that I imagine the woman with the issue of blood yearned to feel in her body, to have in her mind, to have in her home and community. She must have been desperate for a breakthrough and for healing. In Luke 8:43-48, we read her account of having the issue of blood for twelve years. She had already spent the total of her living income on physicians who could not help her. Have you ever felt like no one could help you? At that time, she would have been isolated as a woman in her condition. She would have been set outside of the camp community. Do you know what it is like to be isolated in your suffering? She wasn't allowed to come near other people. When she had heard of Jesus, she pressed through any fear of further rejection, and she reached out in her desperation. She entered the street where Jesus was walking. Her hand grabbed the hem of Jesus's garment with what I call "now faith." Now, in that very moment, she took action with faith. I imagine she knew what was at risk. One of those risks would have been missing the opportunity for her healing. What if she failed? What if someone saw her? What if this Jesus saw her and rebuked her? Take a moment and imagine all the what-ifs that could have arisen in her mind. Her "now faith" said, *What if He can heal me?* It outweighed every other fear.

Do you know what it is like to be isolated in your suffering?

This is what I chose on that day of hiking. I continued to put one foot in front of the other. I trusted that God had invited me to hike the Grand Canyon with Luke and that He would fulfill that promise. But would it be with peace, let alone joy? Only God knew. The current evidence sought to convince me that I was going to fail. I was going to be slow, in pain, and a disappointment to others. The woman with the issue of blood faced evidence that told her she didn't have any hope either.

Pause here and reflect on what evidence you are currently collecting in your mind. Throughout this journey of becoming a woman of peace, begin to recognize repetitive thought patterns, especially those rooted in negativity, doubt, fear, guilt, and shame. What evidence are you collecting about your body? How about the evidence within your current home atmosphere? What does the evidence tell you? Since you picked up this book, I believe it's not currently evidence of peace. Peace may even feel so far out of reach that you cannot imagine it as a possibility for you. What could peace even feel like in your mind, in your body, and/or in your home?

> The current evidence sought to convince me that I was going to fail.

On that trail in 2019, while training to hike the Grand Canyon, I was filled with doubt. God redeemed those moments of doubt in ways I could have never imagined four years later. With sweat pouring down my face, I had navigated through another long journey of battles of pain and fatigue in my body. We had hiked the Grand Canyon in the fall of 2019, and I completed it with a supernatural story. That is a story for another time to be told with Luke.

When we exited the canyon, we entered a spiritual wilderness of sorts. I experienced a lot of loss and pain in the two years that followed—loss of community, friendships, the trust of loved ones, and the ability in my body. With a body that had reached the pinnacle of health, or so I thought, it quickly crashed and returned to familiar conditions from the past. By the fall of 2021, this meant increased pain, digestive issues, nervous system dysregulation, hormone imbalances, and mental battles I still can't fully describe. This battleground is the context for the hike in 2023, when I found myself able to move freely on the Flat Rock hiking trail. It was hard, and yet there was an ease present. Going up the rocky stair climb again and seeing that familiar gravel area of trail, a thought entered my mind that I knew was not my own. God gave me this gift:

"Look at the evidence of healing!"

I hiked that day with peace in a body that, by the world's standards, was in worse physical condition than that of 2019. Luke and I talked and simply enjoyed the silence of being in nature together that day. No lies raced through my mind that Luke was judging me or was frustrated with me. I was at peace! In my body, I moved up the trail peacefully. In my mind, I was simply enjoying the surrounding beauty of nature and the journey. In my marriage, I was at peace that I was moving more slowly. Luke was patiently trekking behind me. Together, we were at peace on this hike.

> There is evidence of healing all around us

There is evidence of healing all around us, friend. We only need to look for it. When you are in the midst of survival, chaos, fear, and turmoil, it will not come naturally at first. Begin to practice your reach. Like the woman in Luke 8, reach! Reach for Truth. Reach for the Truth that there is evidence of healing, evidence of restoration, evidence of ____. Fill in the blank of your prayer request. It's there somewhere in your mind, in your body, and/or in your home. Some days, it may take some effort and may not look as you expect. My body still doesn't look as I thought it would, to be filled with evidence of healing. It is there. I have compiled so much evidence of healing and restoration in my body, my soul, and my home that I can now quickly elevate my perspective back to Truth. Reach and touch the hem of Jesus's garment in your moments of desperation.

"And he said to her, 'Daughter, your faith has made you well; go in peace'" (Luke 8:48).

God is faithful! "May God himself, the God of peace, sanctify you through and through. May your whole spirit, soul, and body be kept blameless at the coming of our Lord Jesus Christ. The one who calls you is faithful, and he will do it" (1 Thess. 5:23-24). In the process of our sanctification, we get to look for the evidence of His faithfulness. Praise the Lord, God is preparing us for His return!

Pause & Pray:

Take a deep breath. Pause and take in your surroundings. From this point forward, through the pause and pray moments, I invite you to take ownership of the prayers. Even though I have written them, be empowered to know you can pray them as your own.

Dear God, I pray for your evidence of healing and restoration to be brought to the light. Every veil of confusion, distortion, or deceit that has been placed in my mind, eyes, and ears be removed in Jesus' name. I pray that my eyes would see, my ears would hear, my nose would smell, my body would feel, and my mouth would proclaim the evidence of your faithfulness. God, may evidence continue to come forth as I journey through these practical applications of looking for your faithfulness. Enlighten me with glimmers of peace increasing in my mind, body, and home as I encounter and abide in you, in Jesus' precious name. Amen.

Elevate Your Perspective and Explore Possibilities:

Are you struggling with a chronic health issue? Recognize today what you are able to do. This is evidence of God's faithfulness. Do you have a relationship that feels strained? Elevate your perspective about them and what they may be going through right now. Come up higher with our good God and explore the possibility that there is a different perspective. Ask God for a Christ-like perspective where you can assume the best. Explore the possibility of how you can bless others versus cursing them in your thoughts or with your words. God is faithful, and you can be faithful to act in kindness.

Ask Questions:

You are welcome to ask questions of God about Himself, yourself, and others. A few questions you may ask after this reading are: "God, why do I continually struggle in this area? Why do I feel such strong emotion about this person's actions? Lord, show me, please? How can I see, feel, or act differently about this circumstance?" Also, how has God already been faithful to you? With this question, create a list of evidence of the faithfulness of God.

Cultivate a Thought:

There is evidence of healing all around me. This statement has become a regular thought in my journey to becoming a woman of peace, and I encourage you to begin practicing this in your own life. Notice how you find what you look for and speak into. As you practice, you will find yourself having moments of simply smiling in thanksgiving as you elevate to a Christ-like perspective.

Embody the Truth:

Sitting or standing, with your eyes open or closed, take a deep breath. In and out. Now slowly, I invite you to pat down your body, starting with your head and using both hands. As you get to your shoulders, I encourage you to cross your arms and pat down the opposite side with each hand, the right hand patting down the left arm and the left hand patting down the right arm. Continue to pat down to your toes and then back up to your head. As you do this gently, I invite you to give thanks for your body. It is good. Even if your body feels broken at this moment, I invite you to see, know, and acknowledge this: it is *your* body. Your body is the temple for the Holy Spirit. God created your body and called it good. Practicing this physical touch and tapping with gratitude is kind. You are a kind and loved daughter of God.

____

Pace Yourself

And I am sure of this, that he who began a good work in you will bring it to completion at the day of Jesus Christ.- Philippians 1:6

TUGGING ON THE ZIPPER, there was no way these shorts were going to fit. At the end of last summer, I could confidently and comfortably wear them. They were evidence of ten months of quiet surrender, obedience, and discipline every time they slid on. But now, yanking them up over my hips and tugging on the zipper, I felt the shame slide on instead. The weight I had lost was creeping back on, and I knew why.

A year and a half prior, I had surrendered the scale to God. At that time, I had no peace in my body's weight, ability, or appearance. With a nagging conviction from the Holy Spirit, I had scheduled an initial consultation with an alternative practitioner. That day marked the beginning of an eleven-month sugar fast — one God invited me into. It wasn't easy to start the fast two weeks before Christmas. My practitioner gifted me with this prayer that helped me thrive those first few months: "Lord, bind my flesh." God prompted me to press into the word "discipline" going into that New Year.

Within a few months, I had found a new rhythm to eating, and a few months later, my body began releasing the weight. By the end of the summer, I was thriving. My energy was good. People were noticing the changes in my body. I was teaching a fitness class at a local shelter. The way I was eating protein and produce, moving my body, and choosing obedience had become a "normal" rhythm of life. I embraced discipline, not as punishment but with purpose. I kept saying, "I get to do this."

Until I didn't.

I surrendered my comfort foods to God for eleven months, until I didn't. I surrendered my movement to Him, until I didn't. One grace-filled decision turned into two, and then ten. Daily compromises were explained as living in a new freedom. I told myself that the way I was eating wasn't sustainable. A compromise became justified in my mind as God's grace being sufficient. His grace is sufficient — that is true. But grace isn't the same as an excuse. I was using the freedom I had found a year and a half ago to abuse that same freedom now. It was evident in the too-small shorts: I had failed again.

His grace is sufficient — that is true. But grace isn't the same as an excuse.

Summer clothing has a way of revealing how much peace

we have in our minds and bodies. Shorts that became a symbol of my pride versus evidence of my discipline now revealed my slide back into shame. The sleeveless tops revealed more than my arms — they exposed my thoughts. Bathing suits? They expose everything we once thought we surrendered to God. I felt guilty. Self-accusations, self-hatred, and self-pity ran deeper than I could even recognize back then. I could only ask: *Why couldn't I do better?*

I didn't want to keep going around this same mountain, physically or spiritually. The Lord's words in Deuteronomy 2:3 spoke to me back then, and they still speak to me today: "You have been traveling around this mountain country long enough. Turn northward." The Israelites left the captivity of Egypt, witnessed the miraculous parting of the Red Sea, and received provision in the wilderness. Yet they seemed stuck wandering and circling Mount Seir. I, too, had experienced freedom from slavery to the scale and sugar addiction. God provided the fruit of weight loss, increased energy, and more. Yet, I remained in the wilderness when I allowed pride to creep in and vanity to become the focus. My "get to" for God became a "get to" for me. Around and around the mountain of wanting peace in my mind and body again, I went.

Like the Israelites, we inherited a promised land to cross into: one that bears the fruit of love, joy, peace, patience, kindness, goodness, faithfulness, gentleness, and self-control. Technically, our promised land is eternal life with God in Heaven. However, I'm taking some liberty here to say evidence of our submission to God is the fruit of the Spirit (Galatians 5:22-23). This is one singular fruit with nine character traits. We are not complete with one and not the others. It's like a piece of Holy Spirit DNA would be missing from our lives.

> The current evidence sought to convince me that I was going to fail.

Praise the Lord, we are continually being perfected until the day of Jesus Christ's return! *The pace of peace is to Pray And Continue Earnestly, or P.A.C.E. yourself abiding in Christ.* I like to think of the ten individuals and two people groups mentioned in Hebrews 11. This chapter highlights the "Hall of Fame" of heroes in the faith. Nineteen times in this chapter, we read the phrase "by faith." These heroes of faith listed were imperfect, broken, fallen sinners who decided to keep going. They are everyday ordinary people, like you and me, who decided to pray and continue earnestly about their Heavenly Father's business. They lived in the Old Testament times before Jesus came, died, was resurrected, and gave us the gift of the Holy Spirit. Imagine the depth of faith they must have had to continue following our currently invisible God. By faith, they prayed and continued earnestly when others misunderstood them, mocked them, slandered their name, talked behind their back, and I imagine much more that remains unlisted.

Suddenly, my shorts not fitting seems pretty insignificant. And praise the Lord, God never leaves us circling the mountain forever. Eight years later, I find myself pulling out my bin of summer clothes as I write this chapter. I'm currently at my heaviest weight, a number I only saw one other time at nine months pregnant. I pull out shorts that I know I should have passed on long ago, giving some to my daughter and others to be donated. It's ironic that a number on the scale that once held shame and guilt is now a hopeful goal. It's a goal submitted to the Lord.

In the midst of trying on clothes that fit last year and having gained even more weight, shame comes knocking. Self-loathing thoughts of how much weight I continue to gain interrupt my day. Disgust creeps in as my stomach folds over some of the shorts' waistlines. I pause. For a moment, I started to circle the all-too-familiar path around the mountain again. Pausing, I pray. I take a few deep breaths and begin to acknowledge the pain my body has stored, and how far I have come to be at peace, no matter the size. This body is good. I smile with compassion, knowing God is with me. Contending for Truth, I thank God that my body is resilient and my mind is continually being renewed. Holding my hand over my chest, I close my eyes and thank God for the breath in my lungs. I feel the rhythm of my heartbeat. Breathing in and out, peace returns as I release the pace of the process of healing and wholeness back to God. I exercise truth through actions of kindness and love to my body now. This looks like taking prayer walks, eat-

There is evidence of healing all around us

ing nourishing foods, strength training, stretching, and other practices that I'll share throughout this book.

Hebrews 11 begins with "NOW FAITH is the assurance of things hoped for, the conviction of things not seen," and recalls the cloud of witnesses that have gone before us. A submitted goal or outcome is in the hands of God. Our responsibility is to live *by faith* and to abide with the Prince of Peace Himself. Will you join me in practicing your "now faith" by pausing, acknowledging, praying, and continuing earnestly today?

Pause & Pray:

(place your hand over your heart and take a deep breath)

Holy Spirit, I invite you to increase my understanding of how I partner with self-hatred, self-accusation, and self-pity. Please open my eyes to how I stay stuck in shame and guilt cycles. Where I have collected evidence that is true to who I am as your daughter, would you bring gentle revelation of Truth when I begin to circle the mountains again? Prompt me to pause, that I may breathe in your kindness and acknowledge the struggle in my mind, body, and home. Remind me to breathe. Grant me the courage to continue with curiosity and to begin to contend and exercise my "now faith." I pray that shame would be released with each exhale as I pray even now. Lord, help me to pray and continue earnestly to move forward with you, the person who is peace. May the fruit of your Spirit become evident in my life in Jesus' name. Amen.

Elevate Your Perspective and Explore Possibilities:

You are a whole person: body, soul, and spirit. Explore the story of your body and how your soul is interwoven in it. Remember, your soul is your mind, will, and emotions. Take note how your mind impacts your body, how your will is in or out of alignment with God's, and how much your emotions rule you. Extend compassion to yourself like you would to your best friend. Invite the Holy Spirit to reveal connections and begin connecting dots of your past with the present condition of your body, soul, and home. Acknowledge what comes to the surface and take note. You don't have to do anything with it today. Breathe and give thanks for the revelation.

Ask Questions:

What do I need to release to the Lord? How am I putting a timeline on God's process for my desires? Are there good things in my life that are no longer God things? Do I need to release these things or simply turn northward as the Lord commanded the Israelites and have God be the focus again?

Cultivate a Thought:

By faith, I will pray and continue earnestly living a life submitted to Christ.

Embody the Truth:

In the midst of setting New Year's goals one year, I attended a prayer meeting. In that meeting, a friend shared a request for a young man to receive a window in a new prison assignment. It would be a miracle if he could be granted access to "the yard" outside. We prayed for favor, and I felt the ache of the Father's heart for this young man. My heart broke at the thought of longing to be granted the privilege of seeing outside, let alone the privilege to go out for a walk. Praying for this man, I received a perspective shift in my goal to get outside for a daily walk: The TRUTH was that it really was a privilege.

Begin to look for pockets of time to get outside during your day. At least once a day, or to begin, maybe once a week, create a time to not only get outside but also take a walk. While you walk, take the opportunity to pray. Prayer is simply a conversation with God. One way you can pray is to observe creation and give thanks to God for it.

Now, when I don't want to exercise my freedom, I think: *It is a privilege to get outside and walk.* To pray and continue to seek the Prince of Peace earnestly is where we discover our pace of peace.

____

____

____

____

With Peace, You are Strong

Pause and Pray

The Lord is my shepherd; I shall not want. He makes me lie down in green pastures. He leads me beside still waters. He restores my soul. He leads me in paths of righteousness for his name's sake. Even though I walk through the valley of the shadow of death, I will fear no evil, for you are with me; your rod and your staff, they comfort me. You prepare a table before me in the presence of my enemies; you anoint my head with oil; my cup overflows. Surely goodness and mercy shall follow me all the days of my life, and I shall dwell in the house of The Lord forever. - Psalm 23:1-6

OUR SON'S CRIES RIPPED ME APART as I lay on my stomach and wept into my pillow. I had just come back to bed after holding and rocking him to sleep. Within seconds, he began wailing again. My body was tired, my mama heart exhausted, and my mind was racing with thoughts that scared me. *I can't keep doing this. I'm a horrible mom for letting him cry and scream. What am I doing wrong? Clearly, what I'm trying isn't working.* The guilt and shame building tension in my body grew louder than the crying in the room next to us. As I heard Zane banging on his crib railing, Luke woke up and asked what I was doing. (I'm not proud of this moment, and I believe not enough moms talk about it.)

I simply said as tears began to surge forth, "I don't know what else to do. I think he is safer in his crib crying right now."

I hated everything about the moment: the crying, the rage surfacing in my mind and body, the defeat, the chaos in my home. A child was simply wanting to be held and comforted, and in my brokenness, I didn't know how to give it to him. I was barely surviving at the moment. My mind was reeling with all the ways I was failing, how I didn't know what to do, and all the advice from other moms on how to get more sleep.

Meanwhile, my body was torn between wanting to nurture this precious life it brought into the world and escape from it. I was getting counseling for the postpartum depression I was battling. Luke helped the best he could with what he knew. The struggle for peace in my mind, my body, and our home was tangible. The weight of the struggle felt like a thick cloud that would come and go unannounced. I hated myself for hiding my face in the pillow while our son cried. At that moment, I forgot who my refuge and my strength was.

Hiding in the metaphorical cave of my pillow, I could only hear the lies and accusations of failing to care for my son. When I think back to moments of desperation when my breath was labored and I was grasping for survival, like that night, I give thanks to God for His mercy. Like David, I was in a cave of sorts. I

I give thanks to God for His mercy.

was hiding the most intense inner struggles from most people because I didn't know who I could trust. Unwarranted advice only compounded the guilt, and I couldn't handle more accusing voices in the middle of the night. For the most part, I appeared well put together in public. I hid the struggle for peace in my mind, body, and home from most of our family and friends. The oppressive darkness of the cave returned with the darkness of the night, and my child, who struggled to sleep. Even in the thick of postpartum depression, I knew deep down my son was not my enemy.

After getting married and having two young children, I became desperate for deliverance. I would cry out to the God of my childhood and reconnect with Him in desperate pleading. In Psalm 142:1, "With my voice I cry out to the Lord; with my voice I plead for mercy to the Lord. I pour out my complaint before him; I tell my trouble before him." David continues through Psalm 142 with a prayer for mercy, a prayer for deliverance from the persecutor, and what I envision as him renewing his mind.

"I cry to you, O Lord; I say 'You are my refuge, my portion in the land of the living" (Psalm 142:5).

I envision David reminding himself during this time of desperation and prayer that God is enough. It's like a heavenly pause in the middle of his prayer to remind his soul that he hadn't forgotten God was with him. David hid in a literal cave—fleeing Saul, abandoned by friends, and overwhelmed by his emotions. I was hiding in a metaphorical one, buried under shame, exhaustion, and silent screams. Maybe you've been there too. Your cave might look like a laundry room breakdown, or hiding in your car in the driveway just to breathe. When our peace is threatened and we find ourselves isolated in a metaphorical cave, I want to remind you that God is our refuge. We get to use our voices to cry out to Him.

How does someone project their voice in the midst of crying out? They take intentional breaths. Speakers and vocalists practice strengthening their lungs, knowing when to pause, to take deep breaths, and the timing of sound and silence to project their voice. I love that Job says, "The Spirit of God has made me, and the breath of the Almighty gives me life" (Job 33:4). Power is found in the pause to breathe. The breath of the Almighty gives us life, and as we read in the last chapter, evidence of the Spirit in our lives includes peace.

Power is found in the pause to breathe.

Breathe, my friend. Take a moment to pause. Close your eyes if you are able and take a few intentional breaths in and out. In this pause, elevate your perspective to the one who gives you the breath in your lungs.

The baby I once feared I couldn't soothe is now a young man. The sleepless nights eventually faded, but the lessons remain as part of my journey in becoming a woman of peace. And now, years later, I find myself in a new time of parenting tension—letting go of control with my daughter, Leah. But now, I recognize the signs when my peace is fading. The Lord has taught me to pause and pray, and in doing so, I find peace much more quickly.

Recently, Leah graduated from high school. She is now an adult navigating decisions about her future, finances, dreams, and desires. The answers to some of these decisions can sometimes seem simple or appear obvious to those of us who have lived a bit longer. However, we all learn from trial and error or from the wisdom of those who have gone before us. Each individual chooses how they will learn in each circumstance. It may be a combination of both.

I am learning how to navigate the tension of giving Leah the space to make decisions on her own and waiting to be asked for my advice. God delivered me from the cave of depression and anxiety. Yet, I can still recognize when depressive or anxious thoughts come for me. In the tension of navigating this season, I get to practice pausing and praying when anxious thoughts arise. Using my mind's eye, I can visualize myself taking refuge in the lap of my Abba, my Heavenly Father. Instead of having my peace stolen, I get to rest in Him (pause) and seek His counsel (pray). My daughter is growing in wisdom, and she has a solid foundation to build her life upon. As I continue to learn how to let go and become a parent of an adult child, I notice I am living in many answered prayers. When I pause and pray, I remember God's faithfulness and become a woman of peace again.

Pause & Pray:

(Pause. Close your eyes and take a few deep breaths first.)

Father God, I pray that your peace would wash over me. Help me to seek refuge in you when the chaos stirs to steal my peace. Prompt and empower me to hide away in you as I embody your word through cleansing deep breaths. I give thanks in knowing that my breath prayers are a sweet aroma to you. Please grant me the physical release of stress in my body as I pause to pray in your presence. Grant me fresh peace from the overwhelm of this world, and may I find solace in the pause to pray in Jesus' name. Amen.

Elevate Your Perspective and Explore Possibilities:

Think about locations in your home, workplace, and daily living that you can reclaim as "peace spots." When you lie in bed, does your mind race and your body fail to rest? How could you use the pause and pray to reclaim this spot with peace? Do you feel anxious in the car, running from activity to activity? Explore the possibility that these areas could become places of refuge versus survival.

Ask Questions:

What repetitive circumstance steals my peace? When I pause, take a deep breath, and pray, how does my body respond? When I pause and pray, how does my perspective shift? How does my prayer life change the atmosphere of my home?

Cultivate a Thought:

God is my refuge and my portion in the land of the living. He is my safe space.

Embody the Truth:

Friend, strength is found in Christ. Embody that strength in your lungs. Take a deep inhaling breath for the count of five. Hold it for the count of three. Then slowly exhale for the count of seven. Consider this your embodied pause to pray. You may also know it as a breath prayer when you couple it with scripture. On the inhale, think or say one line of the passage. On the exhale, finish it or say another short line. For example, let's do a breath prayer with Psalm 142:5. I like to take sections of scripture, or a concept from scripture, and turn it into a breath prayer. From verse five, we will think or say "You are my refuge" on the inhale. Hold. Then, "My portion in the land of the living" on the exhale. Take a moment to try it:

Inhale for the count of five: *You are my refuge.*

Hold for the count of three: *And*

Exhale for the count of seven: *My portion in the land of the living.*

You are not counting at the same time as you are rehearsing the prayer. The timing naturally comes with the words and intention the more you practice breath prayers. You can choose any Bible verse that brings you peace or whatever you need in your current circumstance. Here is another example from Psalm 23:

Inhale: *The Lord is my Shepherd.*

Exhale: *I shall not want.*

Practice with different verses, and you will find favorites that are easy to remember in the midst of chaos and tension. With the breath of life, you are strengthened with peace in the pause to pray.

Elevate Your Perspective

Do not be anxious about anything, but in everything by prayer and supplication with thanksgiving let your requests be made known to God. And the peace of God, which surpasses all understanding, will guard your hearts and your minds in Christ Jesus.
- Philippians 4:6-7

COMPARISON AND JEALOUSY were poised to hijack my thoughts. On what should've been a delightful and simple training hike with my husband, comparison was the thief. Jealousy was the silent killer of connection. The day was our first training hike for the Grand Canyon in eight weeks. Remember the family hike preparing for this training mentioned in chapter one? Hiking has become an opportunity for me to check in with my body's ability and the presence or absence of peace in my soul. On this particular hike, Luke had just returned from Colorado training to become a RevWild Outdoor Leader with Revelation Wellness. For years, I had prayed for this opportunity for him and believed I would get to go with him. However, when the time arrived to sign up, the Lord made it clear that Luke was to go first. I was invited to stay behind at home with the kids and trust God's timing for me. It was a delightful surprise and joy to witness Luke's RevWild training journey; that is, until the week he came home.

My mind was wise enough to tell my mouth to remain shut. I listened to how God showed up and ministered to Luke's heart. Then, I would bring the grief of missing out back to the Lord. I felt at peace with the circumstances until the pictures and stories of others began to show up on social media. I saw the other women in his small group. Many whom I had heard about or knew personally. These are women of faith who are now dear to me. In the days following Luke's return, though, my mind jumped to the thought that *they were better than I was*. These women endured the challenging hike and looked the part: *they were fit and equipped.* The thoughts clouded my mind and my heart as I huffed and puffed up a Pennsylvania hill compared to the mountains in Colorado. Comparison stole the celebration of Luke's freedom in my mind. Jealousy of the other women getting to have this life-altering experience with *my husband* came to kill the connection in our marriage. My heart and mind wrestled internally as my body also wrestled during the hike. The silence felt tangible as I knew my emotions were valid and yet not Truth. We were on the same trail I mentioned in Chapter Two, and as you ap-

Comparison stole the celebration

proach the summit of the overlook, the path becomes nothing but rocks. On this particular day, as we got closer and closer to the summit, a fog slowly settled on the trail. By the time we reached the rock where you could stand to overlook the valley below, there was a thick fog blanketing the area. You couldn't see any of the view or the valley below.

Just because you can't see it right now, the vision is still there. Will you trust me when you can't see the promised land? I heard words something along these lines so clearly in my mind. Words that I knew were not my own. God spoke and gently invited me to trust him. I reached the flat rock and got on my knees. It felt like God had forsaken me in my mind, in my body, and in my marriage.

Worship inaccurately spelled to read WARship is something I did at this moment. It's not always a song. Sometimes the act of worship is a silent surrender, evidenced by the posture I took on my knees. The thick fog surrounded me, and I chose to believe that God's vision for me, for my marriage, and our family was still intact. God would help me break through this battle and get to the other side.

The Lord is my keeper. He is at my right hand. The Lord will keep me from all evil and keep my life. He will keep my going out and my coming in from this time forth and forevermore, paraphrased from Psalm 121. When we remember who is the One that keeps us, who bore the pain of the Cross, and holds space for us in intercession to the Father, we can rise from our place of kneeling on the rock. We can stand up. The vision and promise deposited in our hearts may not be seen today. Pause and pray. Release the emotion to Him. Then stand. Lift up your eyes and remember where your help comes from. It comes from the Lord who made heaven and earth. Remember God's promises woven all through scripture. Isaiah 61:3 is one of my favorites:

Lift up your eyes and remember where your help comes from.

> To grant to those who mourn in Zion—to give them a beautiful headdress instead of ashes, the oil of gladness instead of mourning, the garment of praise instead of a faint spirit; that they may be called oaks of righteousness, the planting of the Lord, that he may be glorified.

Jesus came to give us a beautiful headdress. To keep a headdress on your head, you must hold your head high and upright. As a person in a garment of praise or choir robe who walks with authority, you too, are able to elevate your perspective. Be strong and steady like an oak tree. Raise your limbs in praise and glorify God for who He is and what He has done.

After recently returning to hiking with Luke, we embarked on a new-to-me hiking trail. Almost six years after that tumultuous hike of tension where comparison and jealousy stole my praise, I began to walk. My body now looks less physically capable, my mind is mentally stronger, and my faith is more resilient to move at the pace of peace. I was able to trust God and Luke. It's funny how Satan likes to scheme.

On that early training hike, I fought the lies of being too fat, inflexible, weak, and unattractive. Here I was hiking with a renewed mind, elevating my perspective to the Lord whenever doubt would come knocking. I'd physically look up and remember how good this body has been to me. It found deep joy in strolling, quietly observing the trees, and taking in the sweet aroma of the forest with my newfound peace. I praise God for the resilience of my body to endure heartache and pain. My husband walks beside me or behind me, depending on the width of the trail. He delights in my being with him in the wilderness. It was well with my soul, my body, and my marriage. God gave me a garment of praise instead of a faint spirit.

It was well with my soul, my body, and my marriage.

When overwhelm enters your mind with racing thoughts, your body with a racing heart, and your relationships with tension, reorient your posture. Pause and pray. Invite Him to help you shift your posture to look up to Him. Your Keeper is by your right side. He will keep you from evil. God will keep your going out and your coming in from this time forth and forevermore. Praise the Lord! Pour blessing upon those who desire to persecute you. Renew your mind in God's promises. Collect all the negativity visually in your mind's eyes as you inhale and envision it leaving your body in the exhale, giving it all into God's hands. Release the tension in blessing and praise.

Pause & Pray:

(Take a moment to lift your hands high and look towards the sky. Exhale and Smile.)

Jesus, I praise you! You are faithful and true. I acknowledge that my thoughts and emotions get the best of me at times. Thank you for being quick to help me reorient my posture. May I be known to hold a posture of grace, a posture of seeing the best in others, and in circumstances when I pause and seek your face. Grant me the ability to see with Christ-like vision. Jesus, I look to you for this insight. Lord, thank you for being my keeper and my deliverer in Jesus' name. Amen.

Elevate Your Perspective and Explore Possibilities:

Imagine how your perspective would shift if you started your day in a posture of worship. Explore how you could begin with worship—whether with music, praise and declaration, or thanksgiving. I encourage you to create a playlist of worship songs that remind you of who you are in Christ and shift your eyes to Him. For my playlist of songs, I have named it my "Identity" playlist. It is filled with songs that will quickly remind me where my help comes from and who is my Creator and my delight.

Ask Questions:

What songs and/or Psalms shift my thoughts and eyes towards God swiftly? Where in my life right now do I sense God is inviting me to move my perspective back to Him? Are there any activities or situations that I notice repetitively provoke me towards jealousy or discontent? How can I reorient my days to spend more time in worship or cultivate worship within a daily activity?

Cultivate a Thought:

The Lord is my keeper. He gives me perspective.

Embody the Truth:

Now, I invite you to get your heart beating and your body moving. Whether it's from a chair, clapping and lifting your hands, or full-out dancing, I invite you to let yourself go in the presence of your keeper. If you are able, carve out a pocket of time to be home alone. Hit play on your WARship playlist—songs that reorient your posture to praise. A playlist that reminds you that God is for you, that He is going before you in whatever struggle you are in. Put a smile on your face or release the tears before our good God. Be fully present in your home and in the presence of our Abba, Heavenly Father. Stand firm, and reclaim the Truth that for you and your house, you will serve the Lord (Joshua 24:15). You are positioned with purpose, and no matter what circumstance is currently trying to take your peace, I exhort you to posture yourself in praise. With this new Christ-like perspective, you are equipped with the strength to navigate the struggle.

Ask for Help

But he said to me, "My grace is sufficient for you, for my power is made perfect in weakness." Therefore I will boast all the more gladly of my weaknesses, so that the power of Christ may rest upon me. - 2 Corinthians 12:9

MY SON WAS SIX WEEKS OLD, and I had quit trying to breastfeed him a few days before "the beer can day." We visited the lactation consultants. Zane would latch well to nurse, and then he wouldn't. We circled the same mountain to "get it right," and then his latch hurt me. I felt unbearably sore from him not latching correctly, and I was done. It had been a whirlwind of six weeks. We said goodbye to our 11-year-old dog, our son was born twelve hours later, and within another few weeks, my husband's grandmother passed away.

Our daughter was only four at the time, the time when it all became too much. On this particular day, I don't even know what went wrong. I do know it was at the end of the week when I was taking measures to dry my milk supply. With much prayer and a bit of desperation, I chose to stop trying to breastfeed for my mental health and my husband's connection to our son. The tension of me feeling like a failure, my husband's inability to help me, or to feed our son, was taking a toll in more ways than one. At the time, we had two bedrooms, which meant our children shared a room just big enough for our daughter's twin bed and our newborn son's crib. On this day, they were both in their room crying. From what I can recall, neither of them would take an afternoon nap. Looking back, my daughter may have been crying because of the tension she felt from me. During the few minutes of them crying alone in their room, I sat on the couch in the open kitchen/living area of our single-wide trailer. Tears welled up in my eyes, and I felt completely defeated. Even though the crying only lasted a few minutes, it seemed like an eternity.

Even though the crying only lasted a few minutes, it seemed like an eternity.

After the kids were settled and quietly in their room, my husband came home from work. He found me sitting on the couch on the verge of a breakdown. Luke came to me and picked up the beer can sitting in our middle console. He thought it odd that he had left it there the night before. As he picked it up, he looked at me with confusion and, as I recall, fear. The can was cold. At this point in my life, I don't drink alcohol anymore, especially beer. When I told him that I needed help, he knew at that moment it was bad. What had led me to open a beer? I was doing what I could think of to give myself a time-out and calm my anxious body. No, beer was not the answer. But, in that moment of desperation, I thought maybe a drink would take the edge off of my nerves and bring some calm in the midst of the chaos.

That moment on the couch became a breaking point. I knew I couldn't keep pushing forward alone. I needed help. The Holy Spirit prompted me to ask for help; it wasn't weakness—it was wisdom. In James 4:10, we read that if we humble ourselves before the Lord, He will exalt us. He'll pick us up. At the time, my outlet for gathering with others was found in a Mothers of Preschoolers group. I reached out to a friend and a leader within the group.

The Holy Spirit prompted me to ask for help; it wasn't weakness—it was wisdom.

"Do you know any counselors who could help me and who will work with insurance? When I get an appointment, could you watch my kids for me?"

I knew she took care of children in her home. It was time to get help. Staying stuck in this battle alone wasn't kind to myself, my husband, or my kids. I made the appointment to begin seeking help.

Proverbs 11:14 states, "Where there is no counsel, the people fall; but in the multitude of counselors there is safety." I was falling and needed counsel. As a woman of God, may I encourage you that there is no shame in asking for help. You may believe asking for help means you're failing. But asking for help is brave —a holy act. Sometimes, possibly often, I believe God desires to answer our prayers through other people.

Take a moment and assess the various areas of your life. What is one thing that, if it were taken off your plate, it would lighten your load? Where is there chaos in your thought life, and what would it look like to release that overwhelm in a safe place? Would it be helpful to get a babysitter, ask for marriage counseling, visit your doctor for a physical, or ask an elder to be your mentor or pray for you?

You may believe asking for help means you're failing. But asking for help is brave—a holy act.

Take a deep breath. Pride and shame are not from the Lord. You are not a foolish woman. Look to the Book of Proverbs for wisdom. Proverbs 12:15 states, "the way of a fool is right in his own eyes, but a wise man listens to advice." Likewise, Proverbs 15:22 reminds us, "Without counsel plans fail, but with many advisers they succeed." It's okay for you to release the pride, release the shame, and ask for help.

In his book, *Resilience: Restoring Your Weary Soul in These Turbulent Times*,[1] John Eldredge shares this prayer: "I release everything and everyone to you, Lord." It is a powerful practice and prayer to say. In saying it, what or who are you to release? In the release, what wisdom is the Holy Spirit prompting you to seek? God is our strength. His yoke is light and easy. Let Him carry the weight and train your strength in seeking counsel.

[1]John Eldredge, *Resilience: Restoring Your Weary Soul in These Turbulent Times* (Thomas Nelson, 2022), Audible audio ed., 6 hr., 41 min.

May shame and pride no longer hold you in bondage in Jesus' name. Both almost destroyed the health of my mind and marriage during the first year of my son's life. It was in asking for help that I discovered how dangerous postpartum depression can be. Had I not asked for help, I believe the future lack of sleep would have been even more triggering to my overstimulated, depleted, hormonal body that I shared about in Chapter Four. Sometimes, asking for help starts with a counselor. Other times, it's seeking deeper answers from your body. Both are important and valid. Something I have learned about myself is that for many years, I have most likely had an underactive thyroid. Due to our struggle to conceive our second-born, I knew that my sex hormones were suboptimal. All of this to say, I recently began to ask for more thorough functional lab work. My holistic practitioner agreed it was time to get updated numbers rather than rely on what I had from my family doctor. It is important to note that a continued lack of peace in your mind and/or in your body's condition may have an underlying physiological root cause. In my bloodwork, we discovered lab markers that were suboptimal and one that was significantly low. I am now supporting my body with targeted supplementation and a few further lifestyle changes. Since this discovery, and with the supplementation, I have experienced even greater levels of peace in my body and mind. Sometimes asking for help can mean asking the Lord who you are to ask for wisdom in your healing journey.

Pause & Pray:

(Make a tight fist, squeezing as hard as you can, inhaling as you do. Quickly exhale as you open your hands up.)

Lord, I praise you for meeting me in the midst of my broken heart and chaotic mind, body, and home. I thank you now for bringing calm when the chaos arises. As I just felt the squeeze in my hands and the release of the tension, help me to release everything and everyone I'm trying to hold onto. Control is not serving me well. Give me the courage to be humble. Give me wisdom in when to seek counsel, in what to do, or whom to seek. I pray that I would not look to man for my answers first, because you are my Shepherd, the Light to my path. Increase my trust in you to guide my steps. Please lead me in the way of wisdom to others who may help me in the journey to becoming a woman of peace. Give me the wisdom to discern what support I may need. Wash away any stigmas or shame that may arise. God, be my courage and strength in Jesus' name. Amen.

Elevate Your Perspective and Explore Possibilities:

We are spirit and we are flesh. Up to this point, we have focused on who God is, how you relate to Him, trust Him, and are to seek Him first and foremost. Always. In this space of seeking God first, explore possibilities of what your body may physically need to be at peace. There may be nutritional deficiencies, hormonal imbalances, or other issues that explain some of your lack of peace in your mind and body.

Ask Questions:

Do I find it difficult to ask for help? Why or why not? Is there any evidence in my mood patterns or hormonal cycles that there may be a physiological imbalance present? In my home, where am I most overwhelmed? What could I change, or who could I ask to help lessen the load in this area?

Cultivate a Thought:

With Peace, I can humbly and unashamedly ask for help.

Embody the Truth:

You are stronger than you realize. In your weakness, God is your strength. You get to train strength within you and through you by weight training. Embody the Truth that you are strong in Christ by implementing basic bodyweight strength moves throughout your day. As you elevate your perspective, stand and complete a few squats. When you go to wash your hands or your dishes, place your hands on the counter and step back with your feet. Complete a few elevated or modified pushups. Use your God-given creativity to incorporate a few basic bodyweight strength moves into your daily living activities. Each time you do one of these movements, let it be a declaration: *With Peace Himself, I am strong enough to ask for help.* Your strength isn't in pretending everything's fine—it's in reaching out for support in your weakness. With peace, you are strong.

With Peace, You are Flexible

Cultivate a Thought

"We destroy arguments and every lofty opinion raised against the knowledge of God, and take every thought captive to obey Christ" - 2 Corinthians 10:5

WASHING DISHES AND FEELING the tension in my body, I found my mind processing all these physical sensations in my body. Why was I feeling so tense? Everything in me felt so mad. I felt so angry that I could cry at any moment. My body was clearly trying to tell me something, and I wrestled to figure it out as I washed the dishes. Luke could tell I was mad, or so he thought. He began to question what was wrong. I responded with "nothing" because he hadn't done anything wrong. I stayed mostly silent because I didn't want to say the wrong thing, hurt those in my home, or be misunderstood. Yet, he interpreted my silence as something was very wrong and I was mad. I felt mad, and yet, I wasn't. However, the very thing I didn't want is exactly what happened: I was being misunderstood. My silence in trying to control

I slowly open my hand to explore this objectified word.

the situation led to misunderstanding. In that moment, my thought was, *I am always being misunderstood.* In reality, this thought cultivated actions that led me to be misunderstood. Something had to change—not in my circumstance with Luke asking what was wrong, but in how I was thinking. This is where the Lord reminded me that I get to choose the thoughts I replay in my mind.

In 2 Corinthians 10, Paul instructs the Corinthians to take every thought captive. I picture it in my mind's eye like words coming off a page and grabbing each word with my hand like a child catching a butterfly. Then, I slowly open my hand to explore this objectified word. The object is the thought taken captive and can now be viewed in a logical manner. Like a child will observe and examine the butterfly and its miraculous beauty and structure, we can objectively process thoughts. Paul gave the Philippians the rubric in which we can test these thoughts.

The criteria is found in Philippians 4:8: "Finally, brothers, whatever is true, whatever is honorable, whatever is just, whatever is pure, whatever is lovely, whatever is commendable, if there is any excellence, if there is anything worthy of praise, think about these things." While washing dishes and thinking *I am always misunderstood,* I could choose to process the thought through the Philippians 4:8 filter. Is this thought:

True–aligned with God's Word?

Honorable–worthy of respect?

Just–fair and righteous?

Pure–clean and free from corruption?

Lovely–attractive in God's sight?

Commendable–worthy of imitation?

Excellent–morally and spiritually?

Worthy of praise–stirs up worship and praise?

It was not. Without intention, most of us do not naturally cultivate true, honorable, just, pure, lovely, and commendable thoughts. It takes practice, repetition, and God's Word to renew our minds and thoughts.

Throughout this book, I intentionally end each chapter with a suggested thought to cultivate. The thoughts we cultivate fuel our feelings and how we respond to life. I imagine we have all experienced the evidence of our thoughts becoming verbal. Let us remember that "Death and life are in the power of the tongue, and those who love it will eat its fruits" (Proverbs 18:21). We desire the fruit of the Spirit. While washing the dishes, I filtered the thoughts and feelings of *I am always misunderstood,* and decided once and for all that it be disqualified from taking up space in my mind. Pausing to pray and go through the rubric of Philippians 4:8 regarding how I was feeling, I was able to begin cultivating a new thought: *I may be understood and he still can be for me.* In this thought, I am able to align back to what is true, honorable, just, pure, lovely,

The thoughts we cultivate fuel our feelings and how we respond to life.

commendable, excellent, and praiseworthy about my identity in Christ, as well as Luke's. A thought rooted in God's Truth draws me towards the one I love.

Friend, you do not have to live as a captive to your thoughts. In Christ, you have the authority to take them captive and filter them through His Word, like in Philippians 4:8. Today, you can disqualify what is false and declare what is true. The fruit of your thought life will be peace.

Pause & Pray:

(Take a deep breath. Get an image of a person bringing order to a messy filing cabinet. See this in your mind's eye as you invite God to bring order to your cluttered thoughts.)

Father God, I breathe in your calming presence. Holy Spirit, help me to clear the clutter and bring to mind the one circumstance that, when I intentionally begin to cultivate a new thought, will have the greatest impact. Please release peace in my mind, body, and home as you bring to light the new thought that I can cultivate. I thank you now for the fruit of peace as a result. I thank you in advance that the fruit of peace will be cultivated in my home as well. Jesus, help me to hold space for the in-between of discovering what is, or was, and to what is to be, as I cultivate this new thought. Lord, bring words of wisdom that will shift my mind, to impact my body, and the atmosphere around me in Jesus' name. Amen.

Elevate Your Perspective and Explore Possibilities:

Naturally, we tend to cultivate the negative. We rehearse thoughts in our heads over and over about circumstances and/or people. By now, I hope that you are cultivating a greater awareness of your thoughts. Begin to explore how thoughts form the root of your actions. Try on and explore new thoughts that you can intentionally cultivate using Philippians 4:8 as your filter.

Ask Questions:

What one circumstance in my daily life carries the greatest potential to steal my peace? How do I feel about this circumstance? What thoughts are fueling these feelings? Which actions are happening as a result of these thoughts and feelings? How would I like to feel? What would I like to do instead? What one thought could I cultivate to bring peace to my body, soul, and home as a result? What other Bible verse affirms this thought?

Cultivate a Thought:

I may be misunderstood, and they can still be for me.

Embody the Truth:

Journaling is a powerful tool of embodiment to pour out from your mind through your writing. I hope that you are taking advantage of the space provided in these pages to journal. If you have not, I invite you to start today. Release thoughts through a brain dump of writing down whatever comes to mind about a situation. From here, choose one thought and practice putting it through the rubric of Philippians 4:8. Recognize where you are and then ask God to help you create a new thought for you to renew your mind in Truth. Once you have the new thought, intentionally practice it with movement. When you marry the thought with a Bible passage, you can embrace the opportunity to memorize scripture, too. With cultivation of thoughts and memory work, writing out the thoughts and/or verse multiple times can help. Walking and speaking it aloud offers another powerful option. Let each word of this new thought renew your mind, embody God's Truth, and walk out the peace God's offering in this marriage of the thought and His Word.

Explore Possibilities

For we do not wrestle against flesh and blood, but against the rulers, against the authorities, against the cosmic powers over this present darkness, against the spiritual forces of evil in the heavenly places. - Ephesians 6:12

THREE DIFFERENT TIMES, I sought out therapists. They listened, helped me unravel what was going on in my mind, and processed what was happening in my life. The last counselor I saw brought to my attention the familiar patterns that can run in families. He asked me at the time if I had a strong support network. Did I have a pastor or friends with strong faith who would pray for me in the midst of this journey? At the time, I didn't have that strong support. This counselor helped me process and heal so much that I didn't look for further support or seek to understand these familiar patterns anymore.

In the spring of 2017, I was finally prepared to explore these familiar patterns, also known as generational strongholds, that the counselor had previously mentioned. I had the general understanding of the importance of renewing my mind on Truth, and knew it sometimes required more education. Prayer helped, but I wanted to understand how to have more freedom in my thoughts. I found myself in a season of breakthrough and so much spiritual growth. The patterns of sin in my family tree grew much clearer during this time.

How could I love my extended family with grace and compassion? Like me, they tried to do the best they knew how to do in their own lives. I wanted to understand and experience greater freedom from the patterns resurfacing in my life, primarily in my dreams and thoughts towards others. My heart was not pure, and my soul needed nurturing care. I put into practice that it is okay to ask for help. I reached out to a friend, who was like a spiritual father, and asked him for advice. Who did he recommend, or what program was best to go deeper into soul care? With the list of options I had researched and a two-day wait, he called me back with something that wasn't even on my list.

Getting a pen and paper, he told me to write down the name Mary Buch, who was the lead pastor of a local congregation near him. He gave me her phone number to call and a website to look up. I learned that Pastor Mary wrote the manual, *Spiritual Boot Camp for Overcomers*.[1] Alongside her husband and co-lead pastor, Ron, they taught this message of overcoming. One Saturday a month, they facilitated a workshop to teach and help people get free and stay free from what held them in bondage.

[1]Mary J. Sanchez-Buch, Spiritual Boot Camp for Overcomers (Breakout Ministries, 2013).

After a phone call and a month of waiting for the next workshop, I found myself sitting in my first class of *Spiritual Boot Camp for Overcomers*. Pastors Mary and Ron Buch were both present. I learned that Mary wrote this manual to guide people to Christ and explore *what's on their screen.* She had received this word of "what's on your screen" decades prior to us all holding screens in our hands. It is a metaphor for discerning what is surfacing in our soul. Our soul encompasses our mind, will, and emotions. When something appears on our screen, we get to partner with the Holy Spirit to discern what we are to do. What is He bringing to our attention?

On this particular day, Mary and Ron introduced the concept of soul ties in a way that I had never contemplated before. Through counseling, I was introduced to soul ties in relation to anyone with whom I had any type of sexual interaction. A soul tie is an emotional and spiritual bond that I previously thought only happened when you physically connected with another individual. Pastor Mary expanded with teaching that any time we are in conversation or a relationship with someone, our souls connect. These ties can be a blessing, or in the case of struggles for freedom, they can be like a noose around our neck. Unhealthy soul ties manipulate our mind, will, and emotions from being free of others' thoughts, will, and emotions. My mind was blown. In her manual, she explains there are four key types of strongholds that keep us from

Unhealthy soul ties manipulate our mind

walking in freedom as Spirit-led believers: generational curses/sins, trauma, soul ties, and the demonic.

Generational curses are what initially led me to their boot-camp, and God brought to light the connection of so many puzzle pieces in my soul that felt fractured and manipulated. This began a journey of getting free, staying free, and setting others free as a person who now recognized my part within the strongholds. Friend, you have come so far in this journey of becoming a woman of peace. If something keeps coming to the surface in your mind's eye, explore the possibility that the Holy Spirit is inviting you to a deeper understanding of getting free. To live a life at a pace of peace is to be an overcomer of these strongholds that each of us can have in our lives.

Strongholds are defensive mechanisms. The Merriam-Webster Dictionary[1] defines a stronghold as "a fortified place, a place of security or survival; a place dominated by a particular group or marked by a particular characteristic." In the *Spiritual Boot Camp for Overcomers*, the definition expands even further:

A stronghold is a coping strategy that we use to defend ourselves from the truth. Strongholds are defensive mechanisms that include control, stubbornness, lying, denial, projection, fantasy, emotional isolation, regression, displacement, rationalization, co-dependence, and rejection.

Generational curses are thoughts and behaviors passed on from our ancestors, as mentioned in Exodus 34:6-7. Trauma is living through a deeply distressing or disturbing event. These

[1]Merriam-Webster, s.v. "stronghold," accessed June 18, 2025, https://www.merriam-webster.com/dictionary/stronghold.

events or experiences can paralyze us emotionally, often affecting us physically as well as creating openings of fear and rejection in our lives. Examples from the manual include: fear of rejection, fear of man, poverty or lack, fear of sickness, sexual or mental abuse, sickness or accidents, or situations that continue to haunt us. Soul ties are nets or nooses afflicting our souls with attachments to people, places, or things in the world. Demonic power comes from demon spirits and fallen angels who are influencers from Satan's kingdom.

I will not dive deeper into each of these strongholds here. However, I exhort you to explore the possibility that "what's on your screen" in your mind's eye, dreams, visions, and impressions is an invitation to greater freedom that leads to peace. Freedom and peace are found on a journey with the Holy Spirit. To oversimplify, we can do the following: Recognize the stronghold. Repent for any way we have come into agreement with it. Renounce the curse, the demonic influence, any vows you have come into agreement with, etc. Ask God to forgive you for the sin, forgive yourself, and others. Cut the soul ties associated with the people, places, and things your soul has become "attached" to in the name of Jesus. Replace these now-bound and renounced strongholds with Truth rooted in scripture. You can use the filter of Philippians 4:8 to know you have a solid thought to cultivate.

Freedom and peace are found on a journey with the Holy Spirit

You can also explore the possibility that a recurring thought producing negative fruit might have deeper roots to explore. In the space between the old thought and the new thought you are cultivating, explore the possibility that there may be a stronghold that is keeping you from establishing and replacing the old with Truth.

For example, I meet with a lady who is in need of prayer. She shares that she struggles with sexual sin. Previously, she lived a promiscuous life. I hear her testimony of coming to Christ and how she is overcoming her past. We pray, and I come home. Through the evening, I'm rehearsing what I should or shouldn't have said to her. My soul is tied to what she thinks of me. In the night, I have dreams of when I was promiscuous as a teen. When morning comes, I pause to pray and ask God why I would have this dream. This is something I haven't thought about, dreamed about, or struggled with for years.

The Holy Spirit brings onto "my screen" that I never cut the soul ties that were created with this woman. In Jesus's name, I cut the soul ties to get free. Through the dreams, it is apparent that a familiar spirit is trying to torment me. I renounce it and demand that it must flee in Jesus' name. With Truth, I renew my mind that I am an overcomer through Christ in me. He has paid the price for my sins, and by His blood shed on the cross, I get to be free.

Utilizing the steps found in *Spiritual Boot Camp for Overcomers* is not something you do once and are done. It may be for a particular stronghold or incident. However, we get to daily "bootcamp ourselves" as we discern what is on our screen. I understand this may be introducing to you completely new elements of how we can stay stuck in overwhelming patterns. In the resources section at the end of this book, I have shared where you can get more information if you like. My hope and prayer is that I gave you a foundational awareness of strongholds and how our battle is not against flesh and blood.

we get to daily "bootcamp ourselves" as we discern what is on our screen.

Pause & Pray:

(Take a few deep cleansing breaths. This chapter may have felt overwhelming. Due to the nature of the chapter, I am writing this prayer for you. A prayer for you to receive versus to pray yourself.)

Holy Spirit, I thank you for ministering to my friend reading these words. Thank you that as she read this chapter, you are already bringing to mind strongholds in her life. I pray that she will remember to pause and pray. As she recognizes these strongholds, she elevates her perspective that you are kind. You are bringing this before her for greater freedom and peace. Please highlight or bring into her life a safe person who is led by your Spirit to process, research, and understand it with her. May she be covered in prayer as she explores these possibilities with her friend and/or wise counsel. God, I thank you in advance for the freedom and new thoughts that will be created and embodied moving forward. May she experience a new level of peace in her mind, body, and soul beyond her understanding in Jesus' name. Amen.

Elevate Your Perspective and Explore Possibilities:

We do not give Satan our focus and attention. Keep your eyes on Christ AND explore the possibility that He may highlight areas for greater freedom. Explore the possibility that He has chosen you to be the generational chain breaker.

Ask Questions:

Consider any circumstance with your health: Am I aware of previous generations that had the same issue? When I spend time with someone, am I rehearsing their thoughts or beliefs in my mind? What is coming on my screen? Do I have vivid dreams that could be bringing something on "my screen?"

Cultivate a Thought:

With Holy Spirit, I am strong, flexible, and able to explore the possibility that there is more to my struggle.

Embody the Truth:

Overwhelm is not your portion. Instead of introducing a new embodying practice, take time to practice embodying Truth in ways that I introduced earlier in the book:

Pause & Pray: Practice a breath prayer.

Elevate Your Perspective: WARship in your home with your whole being.

Ask for Help: Train strength in your body.

Cultivate a Thought: Walk and recite aloud a thought you are intentionally cultivating.

Explore the Possibility: You can get free from generational sins.

With Peace Himself, you can begin a generational blessing of becoming a woman of peace and part of a family that is known for being carriers of peace.

____

____

____

____

____

____

____

____

____

____

Navigate the Struggle

But he gives more grace. Therefore it says, "God opposes the proud but gives grace to the humble." Submit yourselves therefore to God. Resist the devil, and he will flee from you.
- James 4:6-7

RIDING IN THE CAR with my husband, I inwardly clench in fear. Hearing the screech of the tires and the collision of metal in my mind, I feel my body tense. I forget to breathe. I hate that I am like this. *Did he see the car ahead of us? Their brake lights were on!* Immediately, I envision us hitting them in the rear end. Luke is a good driver. He would never intentionally put the kids or I in a harmful situation. Through counseling, EMDR therapy, and bootcamping myself, as discussed in the previous chapter, I have grown and matured in my gut reactions. I'm not as quick to call out his name as the fear surfaces, or grab the side of the truck. In this space of being a passenger, I see so much evidence of healing. And yet on this day, my body tells a different story.

My muscles tense when under stress, my heart races,

my breathing becomes shallow, and I'm anything but "at peace" in my body. My mind knows the Truth, but my body reacts in the opposite way. The disconnect becomes visibly evident; you may experience this, too. You have found peace in your mind, in relationships, and have come so far in your own healing. Why does your body still fail you? Under stress, why does it still hold the tension? Why do you do the things you do?

Take a deep breath, friend. Pride may say that it's not true. Shame may say that you know better. Not you. Even after growing so much, knowing God's Word, and recognizing the patterns, you can still feel stuck—stuck in your body and still struggling. We say we love our bodies, but sometimes our reactions reveal deep disgust, disappointment, or even resentment. What if that unspoken tension is blocking our peace? With your mouth, you may recite that you love your body, but in your mind, in your stress, could you actually feel disgust? Everything we've explored so far has been building toward this: learning to navigate struggles not only in our thoughts, but in our bodies, with Peace Himself leading the way.

Pause and pray. Elevate your perspective, and ask others and the Holy Spirit for help. Cultivate a new thought. Recognize any strongholds in your life; renounce, forgive, cut soul ties, and replace with Truth.

Paraphrasing Paul's writings in 2 Timothy 1:3-7, I, too, remember you in prayer as I write these words. I don't know your family of origin or the tears you have cried. In the presence of our Father, I believe that you have a sincere faith. You are a woman of God and great character, and you may also be a person who is tired of the HARD in your life. For this, I have prayed for you, that by this point in our time together, you are experiencing glimmers of peace in increasing measure.

Where there is any struggle, fan into flame the gifts of God that are within you. For Timothy, it was the gift of laying of hands. For you, I encourage you to seek the Lord about your gifts and possibly even take a free online spiritual gifts test if you are not aware of the gifts God has given you. Knowing how God uniquely gifted you can help you stand in your authority and navigate hard moments from a place of purpose.

It is time to navigate the struggle with power, love, and self-control.

It is time to navigate the struggle with power, love, and self-control. Resist the devil who brings about the spirit of fear. Praying 2 Timothy 1:7, a favorite verse of mine, is one way to battle against it: "for God gave us not a spirit of fear but of power, love, and self-control." Merriam-Webster[1] defines self-control as "restraint exercised over one's own impulses, emotions, or desires." Peace is a person, *and* it is an emotion.

I invite you to become further aware of your emotions and how you feel in your body. We have already covered a few practices, such as breath prayers, that implement intentional breathing to help regulate your

Peace is a person, *and* it is an emotion.

[1]Merriam-Webster, s.v. "self-control," accessed June 24, 2025, https://www.merriam-webster.com/dictionary/self-control.

body. Now, let's add a few more practices that may help you embody peace when it feels far away from you in the moment. This peace is found in the pause, prayer, AND embodying God's word through inviting the Holy Spirit into the regulation of your nervous system.

Box breathing is a practice of inhaling for the count of four seconds, holding your breath for four seconds, exhaling for four seconds, and holding your breath for four more seconds. This tool is available to you anywhere and at any time, which is why I love it so much.

Another practice is butterfly hugs, which can be very calming. You may do these with your eyes closed, envisioning God the Father hugging you. Place your right hand over your heart as if you are about to pledge allegiance to the flag. Now place your left hand on the right side of your chest. Hook your thumbs together. Pat your left chest over your heart three times. Now, pat your right chest three times. As you are patting yourself on one side at a time back and forth, take deep and slow breaths. This is a calm bilateral stimulation that lets your body know it is safe.

Taking a walk unplugged from devices, even for just 5-10 minutes, can bring calm to your body. God wired us for peace in our bodies. The thief of this world comes to steal it from us. Navigate struggles by taking your authority back and implementing practices that bring you back to your original design.

God wired us for peace in our bodies.

In the tension of seeing brake lights and my body's initial response to fear, I breathe. I cultivate thoughts rooted in Truth, and I hum. Humming is another nervous system regulator that I intuitively began practicing in challenging situations. It gets us out of fight or flight mode by stimulating the vagus nerve and activating the parasympathetic nervous system to foster peace[1].

It's time to navigate the struggles and bring all the pieces together. With peace, you are flexible to think new thoughts, explore possibilities, and release the struggle. We do not accomplish this by a strong arm or willpower alone. You are a daughter of God. Stand firm. Resist the devil. Receive God's grace and move forward.

Recognizing the tension in my body and how quickly I flinched, I prayed, "God, we have eight hours to drive. It is not fair to Luke or the kids for me to get stuck in this fear response." Asking for His help, I cultivated a thought: *With Christ, I am at peace*. Repeating it in the form of a breath prayer: Breathe in *"With Christ,"* and exhale "*I am at peace*." Again, *"With Christ, I am at peace*." I close my eyes. I recognize that my flesh has begun to partner with a spirit of fear.

God, forgive me. I repent for coming into agreement with this fear. In Jesus' name, fear you must flee! With You, Lord, I am at peace. I believe You are giving me the peace to not only resist the temptation to partner with fear and steal the joy of this road trip, but You will grant me the peace that will let me sleep in Jesus' name. Amen.

[1] Jana Joshu Grimm, *Total Health Revival Program* (2025), https://www.drjana.com/GroupProgram (subscription required).

In quiet and repetitive breath prayers, my mind is renewed to Truth, my body leans into peace to sleep for a bit, and peace rests upon the "home" of the truck for my family. Satan no longer has a hold of me!

Pause & Pray:

Father God, I pray that when a physical situation arises that brings tension and fear within my body, would you bring to light the root? Guide me in navigating the fear and using the practices that I have been taught here. Would you please bring to memory evidence of ways that I have already implemented practices within this journey? May I take a moment to pause, reflect, and be filled with gratitude for what you are teaching me in becoming a woman of peace in Jesus' name? Amen.

Explore Possibilities:

What if your body isn't broken, but beautifully wired to alert you when something feels off? What if God is inviting you to partner with Him in peace—not just in your mind, but in your breath, your heart rate, your posture? Explore the possibility of how these shifts will impact the atmosphere around you, too. Consider how you can add one practice to your daily rhythms to stay grounded in Christ through your nervous system.

Ask Questions:

What circumstances tend to trigger fear in me? What thoughts am I having? Do any memories arise with fear? Which practices of peace grounded and rooted me in Christ in the past? How is God inviting me into deeper healing within not only my thoughts, but also in my body and home?

Cultivate a Thought:

With Christ, I am at peace.

Embody the Truth:

Take a few minutes today to walk and breathe with intention. Inhale slowly and say: *"With Christ"*... Exhale: *"I am at peace."* As you walk, practice humming. Let the humming bring your body into the present as you also look at the nature around you. God's creation moves in seasons and rhythms, and so do we. Our body is for us, and we have the Holy Spirit within us. In Christ, you are safe. You are loved. With the Prince of Peace, you get to embody peace.

With Peace, You are Able

Practice Daily

But be doers of the word, and not hearers only, deceiving yourselves. - James 1:22

KEEPING PLANTS ALIVE is not my greatest gift. While gardening should come naturally with my family's agricultural background, it does not come naturally to me. One year, we rototilled a section of the yard, fertilized the soil, sectioned off the square plots, and planted seeds. I envisioned delicious tomatoes, zucchini, and squash come harvest time. In reality, I was scouring the internet for ways to keep the plants alive. *Why did the leaves have this odd discoloration?* It clearly wasn't normal, and I tried everything: watering more, watering less, and nothing seemed to solve the problem. Armed with a picture of zucchini (or was it summer squash?) on my phone, I went to the one whom I was confident could help: my grandmother. In my childhood, I remembered her and my grandfather having a prolific garden. She asked about my garden adventure, and this became my opportunity to seek her help. However, when I showed her this mysterious plant activity, she laughed.

"Never in my life have I seen anything like that!"

The plant died and didn't bear fruit. I never discovered what went wrong that year. I'm not even certain if it was my zucchini plants. Either way, my gardening attempt failed.

Years later, my mentor and friend, Alisa Keeton, taught this acronym to me within the Revelation Wellness community: F.A.I.L.: **There are no failures in the Kingdom, only Frequent Attempts In Learning**. It's a beautiful acronym that reminds me of God's grace and continuous redemptive work: "And the God of all grace, who called you to His eternal glory in Christ, after you have suffered a little while, will himself restore you and make you strong, firm, and steadfast" (1 Peter 5:10).

When an arborist plants a magnolia tree seed, germination of the seed requires months and proper preparation. Once the seed germinates and sprouts, the sapling will only grow maybe a foot tall, at most three. For the first few years, this tiny tree may appear to be a failure with this slow growth. However, the magnolia tree uses its energy in those early years to establish a strong root system. It can take ten to twenty years for a magnolia tree to reach full maturity. When I learned about this, I realized that the process of sanctification in becoming a woman of peace parallels the tree.

You may fail sometimes at keeping your peace. Your

mind may race with anxious thoughts, or your body may tense when something attempts to steal your peace. It's okay if you fail. You are learning! Remember, peace is not only a feeling. Peace is a person. Christ will reach out His hand and invite you to stand back up, to look up. His grace will restore you and strengthen you in the learning process of becoming a woman of peace. Keep learning and letting the Holy Spirit course correct you each day. I used to write prayers for peace in my journal frequently; now I give thanks for how God has helped me navigate struggles with peace. Some days, I still "fail" and get to learn how I could have been a doer of the Word versus being of the World.

Keep learning and letting the Holy Spirit course correct you each day.

Decide how you will continue to implement the practices you have learned throughout this book. Each time you pause to pray before acting, you will retrain your brain to react in peace. When you reorient your posture to elevate your perspective, you learn new ways of worship. Asking for help keeps you humble as you acknowledge your weaknesses. Cultivating new thoughts brings change in how you approach circumstances, one step at a time. Exploring the possibility that some struggles are beyond your flesh and blood brings freedom that shifts not only your soul but also the atmosphere. Navigate the struggles you feel within your good body and find yourself at ease where tension once ruled.

You are not who you were when you began this book.

Let's pause and praise God for the promise in Lamentations 3:22-23: "The steadfast love of the Lord never ceases; his mercies never come to an end; they are new every morning; great is your faithfulness." God is good! Continue to trust the process of becoming. Replace the lie that you failed and rejoice that you have been given a new day to attempt to learn again! I invite you to place this verse on a sticky note on your bathroom mirror. Consider beginning your day with thankfulness for a new day to practice, a new day in becoming a woman of peace.

> Continue to trust the process of becoming.

Like my experience with gardening, our lives won't always produce the fruit of love, joy, peace, patience, kindness, goodness, faithfulness, and self-control. Through the years, I have continued to practice my gardening skills. I am still far from being someone to offer advice in that area, but I've improved. The fruit comes forth more by God's grace than my sheer effort or knowledge. However, I have learned over time that certain types of leaf discolorations mean over-watering, while others point to a nutrient deficiency, and others to a root system problem. Frequently, I attempt to learn when a plant doesn't produce fruit as it should. Whether becoming a master gardener or a woman of peace, we become through practice.

Pause & Pray:

God, you are faithful to give me frequent attempts in learning, and for that I am so grateful. May I pace myself each day to continue to move forward in the process of becoming. Thank you for your grace, and may I continually practice being a doer of your Word—a woman of peace that is becoming more like Peace Himself. I pray that the way I live my life would teach others that it's okay to fail. May I model that in failure, I choose not to stay stuck, but get back up, learn, and take another attempt. Thank you, that in the frequent attempts in learning, I will become a woman of peace in Jesus' name. Amen.

Elevate Your Perspective and Explore Possibilities:

You yelled at your kid again. The driver tailgating you brought rage to the surface. Your husband forgot an important date. Whatever the circumstance stealing your peace, come up higher. Pause and be with God in prayer. Then, explore the possibilities of why you failed to keep your peace. Acknowledge what happened. Consider why you reacted the way you did with no shame or condemnation. Then, exercise your faith to attempt to shift your reactions and actions next time from what you learned.

Ask Questions:

How can I practice being at peace today? What does peace feel like in my body? What are my thoughts when I am at peace? With the embodiment tools in my "peace toolbox," how can I practice being a woman of peace today?

Cultivate a Thought:

There are no failures in the Kingdom, only frequent attempts in learning.

Embody the Truth:

Becoming a woman of peace happens with rhythms of renewal. Rest is essential for your body, your soul, and for you to be fully available in your home. To be still and be loved by our Lord, especially when we feel like we are failing, is essential. Play a soothing worship song, an audio Bible recording, or a "Pause & Pray" episode on my podcast, *The Pace of Peace*.

In lying down on the floor or sitting in an upright chair, relax your shoulders, maybe move your neck gently side to side. Allow yourself to be present in your body. Once settled, be still. Let the worship music or an audio recording fill the air. Invite God into the space to be with you and minister to you. With each breath, be still and present to Peace Himself, who abides in you and through you.

Include Your Family

...but as for me and my house,
we will serve the Lord. - Joshua 24:15

EACH DAY, YOU PRACTICE waking up earlier, praying, journaling, taking walks, strength training, and seeking Jesus, but the chaos in your home still crashes into you. The overwhelm and frustration settle in. Your husband doesn't "get" what you're doing. The kids keep interrupting your Bible and/or workout time. Instead of *being* a person of peace, you feel like you're fighting to keep your peace.

Maybe you find yourself thinking: *I'm doing all this for them, Lord... why does it feel like they're against me?*

More times than I can count, I've tried to build a new habit, only to be met with frustration. Wanting to read my Bible and journal consistently? A kid suddenly shifts their sleep schedule or interrupts with questions about the day. Wanting to take a walk in silence? A family member invites themself or my phone rings with an important call. Walks have become my favorite way to get in my body, feel, and release my thoughts and emotions to the Lord over the last few years. Often, these walks are to listen to or respond to a friend's voice memo. Including my family in these sacred spaces was something I often resisted. I thought peace was something I had to protect at all costs, and Jesus' life reminds me it's a relationship to steward.

True peace isn't something we guard and hoard

True peace isn't something we guard and hoard—remember peace is a person. Christ in us gives us peace. His presence is meant to be shared. We desire to model Jesus to the world and invite others to know Him through the way we live. When I become frustrated or overwhelmed by something I'm doing, I forget to first include Peace Himself. Secondly, I forget that I get to be a thermostat of peace in my home, not a thermometer of frustration and overwhelm.

Friend, you are not on this journey of peace alone. The practices and transformation God is doing in you are intended to be shared, modeled, and extended to your family. You get to bring peace *home*, and you don't have to carry that responsibility alone. Invite your spouse and kids into these practices; put on your new self as Paul exhorts the Colossians in Chapter 3. Even if your family doesn't fully understand or believe yet, modeling peace can plant seeds that grow over time. Paul's words are not just lofty ideals. They meet us in the daily grind of short tempers and interrupted walks.

"Put on then, as God's chosen ones, holy and beloved, compassionate hearts, kindness, humility, meekness, and patience, *bearing with one another* and, if one has a complaint against another, *forgiving each other*; as the Lord has forgiven you, so you also must forgive. And above all these *put on love*, which binds everything together in *perfect harmony*. And *let the peace of Christ rule* in your hearts, to which indeed you were called in one body. And *be thankful*." (Colossians 3:12-15)

With patience and kindness, I continue to forgive myself for the way I have been selfish. I ask forgiveness of my husband for being silent in frustration or being short with a child. Putting on love and the peace of Christ within me, I pause and pray. Before I go on a walk, I ask myself if I need the time alone or if I can invite my family to go with me. What are my thoughts? Could it be possible that this time I could focus on them? I find myself including them in a walk to talk and connect. Stretching before bed? I get to be at peace as I work through the tense parts of my body. Now, a grown child is learning to work the tension out alongside me.

The Israelites would travel to Jerusalem for the annual festivals, like Passover, together as a family. Psalms 120-134 were used as they journeyed to these festivals for reflection, worship, remembering God's faithfulness, and promises. I imagine it was a joyful time of being together as they walked and sang these beautiful psalms. We, too, can make our homes places where worship and peace are carried on the journey. May Psalm 128 encourage you, titled "Blessed is Everyone Who Fears the Lord":

> We, too, can make our homes places where worship and peace are carried on the journey.

"Blessed is everyone who fears the LORD, who walks in his ways!

You shall eat the fruit of the labor of your hands; you shall be blessed, and it shall be well with you.

Your wife will be like a fruitful vine within your house; your children will be like olive shoots around your table. Behold, thus shall the man be blessed who fears the LORD.

The LORD bless you from Zion!

May you see the prosperity of Jerusalem all the days of your life!

May you see your children's children!

Peace be upon Israel!"

Pause & Pray:

(Take a deep breath. Get an image of your family in your mind's eye.)

Father God, from whom every family comes, I thank you for an increase in compassion, kindness, humility, meekness, and patience. May my heart be softened wherever unforgiveness, bitterness, and/or resentment have taken root. I am a beloved daughter of yours, and I pray in the remembrance of how you freely forgive me, I, too, can forgive in Jesus' name. May your Spirit move through my home, to bring unity, salvation where there is unbelief, and the peace that passes understanding. The peace that only you can bring to not only me, but also my home. Lord, do what only you can do first in my soul and then through me to others in Jesus' name. Amen.

Elevate Your Perspective and Explore Possibilities:

Consider those in your home. Without judgment and with compassion, ask God to help you see them as He sees them today. What would He see and/or know that you may look right past? Are they sleeping well? Eating well? Is work stressful for your husband right now? Are the kids' love tanks full? A mentor once taught me to explore the possibility that giving away the very thing your heart needs may be the answer to your prayer.

Ask Questions:

Am I guarding and hoarding my peace? Have I gotten fixated on maintaining the *feeling* of peace versus being with the person who is Peace, Christ? How can I invite my family into the practices that I have learned? Could these practices help my husband and/or child(ren)?

Cultivate a Thought:

With peace, I am a safe place for my family.

Embody Truth:

It's a gift to become aware of your thoughts, how you feel in your body, and to put language to these thoughts and feelings. What if your family joined you on this journey—not perfectly, but little by little? What if your car became a place for prayer pauses, your living room a place of breath prayers, your movement an act of worship together? Consider ways you can begin to include your family in these practices. Try using language to communicate with your family what you are doing and why. Invite them to pause and pray. Teach them a breath prayer. Let them see the thought you are cultivating on the refrigerator instead of your bathroom mirror. Tell stories of how you have overcome a generational struggle that you believe will stop with you. Invite them on a walk where you talk together and pray for your family and neighbors. Peace is not something you hoard; it is Christ—Peace Himself, you strive to be like.

Embrace Your Pace

You keep him in perfect peace whose mind is stayed on you, because he trusts in you. - Isaiah 26:3

WE HAD DONE IT! Luke and I had hiked the Grand Canyon rim to rim in one day: from the north rim down to the river and out the south rim. The training was intense leading up to the day of the big hike, and I faced battles within my mind, my will, my emotions, my body, and our marriage. I entered the canyon with the prayer I had prayed for months prior, "Lord, may I experience peace and joy in the canyon, please?" In other words, could the canyon be "easy" after all these trials? On the other side, God answered the prayer! It was far from easy. But the Holy Spirit was my strength, my body was able, and my mind was set upon Christ's promise, "With the Holy Spirit, I was strong, flexible, and able." Life felt good. I found a rhythm to our days, extending kindness to my body through nourishment, training, educating my kids at home, and being active in our local body of believers. I felt like I was winning. I had experienced a dream and a promise fulfilled. The Lord was faithful in this season of endurance and training.

Except the season of enduring isn't promised to cease. In an earlier chapter, we read about the heroes of the faith found in Hebrews 11. Hebrews 12 begins with the word "therefore," connecting it to the great faith heroes in Chapter 11. These heroes weren't perfect, but they *endured* by keeping their eyes on God's promises. By faith, they endured and continued their unique race of life. Just like them, we are called to run our race with endurance.

"...let us also lay aside every weight, and sin which clings so closely, and let us run with endurance the race that is set before us, **looking to Jesus**, the founder and perfecter of our faith, who for the joy that was set before him endured the cross, despising the shame, and is seated at the right hand of the throne of God." (Hebrews 12:1–2)

this discipline isn't punishment—it's love.

This race we are in, it's a daily walk of peace, not a sprint. It's a lifelong pace of peace: a race of endurance. Hebrews 12 continues with a message that may feel challenging at first: discipline. But this discipline isn't punishment—it's love. It's refinement. God is actively fathering you.

"My son, do not regard lightly the discipline of the Lord, nor be weary when reproved by him. For the Lord disciplines the one he loves, and chastises every son whom he receives" (Hebrews 12:6-7).

The pace of peace is one of abiding in Christ. It is found in being a doer of His word. Peace is submitting your whole self to the Lord for refining and refreshing. You are His daughter, and He lovingly shapes you through every struggle, stress, and surrendered moment. Your pain is not pointless. Your training is not wasted. As Hebrews 12:11 says:

"For the moment all discipline seems painful rather than pleasant, but later it yields the **peaceful fruit of righteousness** to those who have been trained by it."

Isn't this what we have been cultivating? Peace. Righteousness. Strength in Christ. We do not earn these things. We receive this fruit of peace, righteousness, and strength as we abide in Christ through the highs and lows of life.

Hebrews 12 finishes with a reminder of how there will be a great shaking, where all that can be shaken will fall away.

"Therefore let us be grateful for receiving a kingdom that cannot be shaken, and thus let us offer to God acceptable worship, with reverence and awe, for our God is a consuming fire" (Hebrews 12:28). When your day does not go as planned, a family member is at odds with you, or your body is in dysfunction, you can choose to abide. Invite the Prince of Peace to refine, to discipline, and direct you. In His presence, you become more like Christ.

In Christ, you become at peace, for He is peace. You become unshakeable. Be kind to yourself. Notice your wins and the patterns of those wins. Let the dots connect that highlight your unique pace of peace to pause, acknowledge, contend, and exercise your faith, to be a doer of the Word—body, soul, and home.

Let the dots connect that highlight your unique pace of peace

Most nights, as I prepare for bed, I check the app that I currently use for my workout plan. *What is the workout of the day tomorrow?* This daily movement has become a joy and something I look forward to most days. Then, I will open my notes app and make a rough draft of the next day's schedule to include my "peace practices." With practice and continual modification over the years, I discovered a pace of peace in my body, in my soul, and in my home. This pace looks like waking up, eating breakfast, reading the Bible, completing the workout of the day, walking outside or on the treadmill, maybe making a protein drink, getting ready for the day, and journaling, if time permits. This is how I typically start my days with Jesus and Peace Himself in this season of life in order to be at peace in my mind and body. I know it would look different if my kids were little or if I had grandchildren visiting. We get to continue to practice and adjust our daily rhythms—our peace practices—to what works today. How I pause and pray today looks different from how I paused and prayed while holding a crying baby.

The thing I have come to know is that when I'm at peace in my mind and body, greater peace is available in my home. As a woman of peace, struggles will still occur. When we abide in Christ, Peace Himself, the shaking ceases to steal our peace. There is evidence of Christ's faithfulness, as seen through the countless stories of situations that once would have wreaked havoc within me. Now, I am tested, but no longer shaken. I am a woman of peace abiding in Peace Himself, Jesus Christ. And, friend, this same truth is for you. Each pause, each prayer, each small adjustment you make in practicing peace is shaping you into a woman who carries peace wherever she goes. This is the evidence of Christ's faithfulness in you—the storms may come, but Peace remains.

Pause & Pray:

(Deep breath. Smile.)

God, you are here. With you, I am in awe and wonder. You are faithful and everlasting. I feel your delight and pride. Please continue to prompt me to make small adjustments in becoming a woman of peace. You are my everything, my everlasting, never-failing me Father: my Abba. I give thanks for knowing you take delight in disciplining and guiding me. Please continue to bless me with strength, flexibility, and ability by your Spirit to discover my unique pace of peace, in Jesus' name. Amen.

Elevate Your Perspective and Explore Possibilities:

You have permission to dream again! Explore the possibilities of what it means for you to be a woman of peace abiding in Christ. At peace, what are the possibilities? What can you do now that you couldn't or wouldn't before? Imagine. Dream. Ask God to give you a vision of how your peace can shift atmospheres around you. Explore the possibility of how, when you are at peace, you get to let others meet Peace Himself.

Ask Questions:

How has my relationship with God—Father, Son, and Holy Spirit—shifted since starting to discover my pace of peace? Where do I see evidence that I am becoming a woman of peace? In what way have I prayed and continued by faith? When did I most recently pause and pray to breathe and be with the Lord in the moment? In what ways have I seen an opportunity to elevate my perspective and worship despite warfare? Who have I asked to help me with the overwhelm? What new thoughts do I find myself starting to think naturally? What stronghold has been revealed and released, where I am now free? What rhythms or practices embodying the Truth have I begun to implement? Who is my person or my people that are safe to invite into my journey? What does it mean for me to live at the pace of peace, as a woman of peace abiding in Christ today?

Cultivate a Thought:

With Holy Spirit, I am strong, flexible, and able to be a woman of peace. When I abide in Christ, I am at peace.

Embody the Truth:

I pray the sun is shining on this day. Whether it is or not, the SON is shining upon you. You haven't arrived at a Promised Land, but you have been becoming a woman of peace. If you are able, step outside, feel the sun on your face, and let it shine upon you. Embody the Truth that The SON, Jesus Christ, is shining upon you with joy. In this world, you will have tribulation, but with Peace Himself, you are equipped to embody Truth, bearing fruit of love, joy, peace, patience, kindness, goodness, faithfulness, gentleness, and self-control. Pray and continue earnestly, seeking God first, and He will help you be at peace.

You have not arrived at a destination, but you are becoming someone new. You are now a woman who knows how to pause and pray. A woman who can elevate her perspective to be more like Christ. A woman who asks for help. A woman who cultivates thoughts that are true, honorable, just, pure, lovely, commendable, and praiseworthy. A woman who explores possibilities and practices abiding in Christ daily. You are not just surviving anymore. You are living at the pace of peace—with Christ, in Christ, and for Christ.

Now go. Be a woman of peace in your body, your soul, your home, and your community. Let Peace Himself flow through you into every atmosphere you enter. You are strong. You are flexible and able to navigate whatever comes your way with Peace. You are a daughter of The King, the King of an unshakeable Kingdom—and this is only the beginning.

Acknowledgments

FIRST AND FOREMOST, I give thanks to God: Father, Son, and Holy Spirit. Without the grace and peace of my Savior, I would not be who I am today or have had the ability to write this book.

To Luke, the love of my life: "God blessed the broken road that led me straight to you," as the Rascal Flatts' song goes. It is still as true as when we had our first dance as husband and wife. You are unwavering in your commitment to love and cherish me through richer and poorer, in sickness and health, through all the highs and lows. Thank you for continually believing in me and supporting me.

My precious kids, Leah and Zane, who taught me patience and love in ways I never knew. I am so proud of the young adults you have become. May you continue to love, trust, and follow our Heavenly Father. He is faithful. There is so much evidence of His faithfulness to me in each of you.

To my parents, Leroy and Brenda Walker, thank you for modeling and teaching me resilience, work ethic, and that "Dreams Happen" when you continually seek God, take risks, and get back up when you fail.

I am grateful for all the friends who listened, prayed, and stuck by me through this process. Kim Whitehill, you never once wavered in believing in me, encouraging me, and praying for me. Laura Moore, you sat with me in some of the darkest days and encouraged me to embrace the "crazy." You recognized that the "crazy" was the Holy Spirit at work within me. Heather Johnson, you prayed me into Revelation Wellness as my enrollment advisor and then became one of my dearest friends. You are a friend who calls the gold out of me and grinds the rough edges away with Truth, all packaged in love. Britney Shoemaker, you give me permission to explore possibilities with Holy Spirit, hold me accountable to growth, and encourage me to flourish in all the ways. Beth Sloan, the friend for whom I prayed. You are like the older sister I could have only dreamed of, who gets the way God wired me, and speaks wisdom into every weary place of my soul at just the right time.

The influence of my mentors over the years has not only shaped this book, but also my life in becoming a woman of peace. Ron and Mary Buch, your prayers, wisdom, and teachings continue to help me live the life of a believer that is marked by overcoming. Nathan Herndon, you called out the lie that I was not crazy all those years ago. It was a turning point I will never forget—the day I recognized the lie and began to embrace the gifts God gave me. Don Hoover, thank you for being the spiritual father I didn't know I needed.

A special thank you to my mentor and friend, Alisa Keeton, the founder of Revelation Wellness. You took a risk on a Word that interrupted a schedule and forever changed my life.

Ten years later, you have been my leader, my mentor, and my boss through various seasons. One thing remains beyond any role: you are my big sister in Christ who radically loves Jesus. You continually inspire and challenge me to keep my eyes upon Him. There are not enough words—thank you.

This book would not have become a reality without my writing coach, Nika Maples. Thank you for coaching me through mindset blocks and every step of this process. To all of the Anointed Writers' community, thank you for holding space for me during coaching calls, continually encouraging me, sharing your expertise, and insight through this journey.

To my Revelation Wellness family, thank you for being "home" to me. I especially want to thank those who served on the prayer team when it was time for me to press into this calling. You sent me with prayers, words, encouragement, and gifts that healed parts of my soul that I can't repay you. I am so grateful.

Thank you to the professionals who helped carry this project across the finish line. To my editor, Kerry Harger, your spiritual and editorial eyes were a gift of peace in this process that God knew was for such a time as this. To Brad Pauquette, Allie Prince, and the designers at The Company, thank you for putting the final touches on this for print.

Finally, to you, the reader: thank you for inviting me into your life. When overwhelm comes, may you know you are never truly alone.

Resources

Come back anytime—this page will grow with new tools and encouragement just for you.

https://www.michellebrumgard.com/popresources

About the Author

MICHELLE BRUMGARD IS AN AUTHOR, speaker, and coach who helps women discover calm in the midst of life's chaos—whether in their body, soul, or home. A certified Health Coach through the Institute of Integrative Nutrition and a Certified Revelation Wellness® Instructor, she brings a unique blend of practical tools, biblical truth, and Spirit-led encouragement.

Michelle is also a pioneer of prayer ministry, having served in both the local church and a non-profit organization, where she witnessed firsthand the power of God to heal hearts and restore lives. Her own journey through valleys of overwhelm, anxiety, depression, and chronic health issues has led her to embrace a slower, Holy Spirit-led way of living she calls the pace of peace. Out of that journey, she now serves as a safe place for women to be real, learn new rhythms, and encounter the transforming presence of Christ.

As host of The Pace of Peace podcast, Michelle invites listeners to step away from the noise of the world and lean into God's invitation to walk with Him at His pace. Whether teaching, coaching, or speaking, her foundation is always intimacy with the Lord and relationship with Him as the source of true peace.

Michelle lives in South Central Pennsylvania with her husband, Luke, and their two children, whom she has home-educated. She loves quiet mornings, outdoor walks, Scripture, and helping women exchange overwhelm for peace. You can connect with her at www.michellebrumgard.com.

www.ingramcontent.com/pod-product-compliance
Lightning Source LLC
Chambersburg PA
CBHW020419150626
46554CB00014B/1947

* 9 7 9 8 9 9 3 2 7 5 3 0 7 *